PENGUIN BOOKS — GREAT FOOD

The Pleasures of the Table

JEAN ANTHELME BRILLAT-SAVARIN (1755–1826) was a French lawyer and politician, whose book *The Physiology of Taste*, published in 1825, is still inspiring chefs and food enthusiasts alike, particularly through his essay 'On Gourmandism'. It contains some of the most famous dinner-table witticisms and aphorisms in history, including 'Tell me what you eat, and I will tell you what you are.'

The Pleasures
of the Table

JEAN-ANTHELME BRILLAT-SAVARIN

Translated by Anne Drayton

PENGUIN BOOKS

PENGUIN BOOKS

Published by the Penguin Group
Penguin Books Ltd, 80 Strand, London WC2R 0RL, England
Penguin Group (USA) Inc., 375 Hudson Street, New York, New York 10014, USA
Penguin Group (Canada), 90 Eglinton Avenue East, Suite 700, Toronto, Ontario,
Canada M4P 2Y3 (a division of Pearson Penguin Canada Inc.)
Penguin Ireland, 25 St Stephen's Green, Dublin 2, Ireland
(a division of Penguin Books Ltd)
Penguin Group (Australia), 250 Camberwell Road,
Camberwell, Victoria 3124, Australia
(a division of Pearson Australia Group Pty Ltd)
Penguin Books India Pvt Ltd, 11 Community Centre,
Panchsheel Park, New Delhi – 110 017, India
Penguin Group (NZ), 67 Apollo Drive, Rosedale, Auckland 0632, New Zealand
(a division of Pearson New Zealand Ltd)
Penguin Books (South Africa) (Pty) Ltd, 24 Sturdee Avenue,
Rosebank, Johannesburg 2196, South Africa

Penguin Books Ltd, Registered Offices: 80 Strand, London WC2R 0RL, England

www.penguin.com

La Physiologie du goût first published 1825
This translation, *The Philosopher in the Kitchen*, first published in Penguin Books 1970
This extract published in Penguin Books 2011
This edition published for The Book People Ltd, 2011
Hall Wood Avenue, Haydock, St Helens, WA11 9UL
1

All rights reserved

Set in 10.75/13pt Berkeley Oldstyle Book
Typeset by Jouve (UK), Milton Keynes
Printed in Great Britain by Clays Ltd, St Ives plc

Cover design based on a pattern from a plate by Sevres Porcelain Factory,
eighteenth century. (Photograph copyright © White Images/Scala Florence.)
Picture research by Samantha Johnson. Lettering by Stephen Raw

Except in the United States of America, this book is sold subject
to the condition that it shall not, by way of trade or otherwise, be lent,
re-sold, hired out, or otherwise circulated without the publisher's prior
consent in any form of binding or cover other than that in which it is
published and without a similar condition including this condition
being imposed on the subsequent purchaser

ISBN 978-0-241-96067-7

www.greenpenguin.co.uk

MIX
Paper from
responsible sources
FSC® C018179
www.fsc.org

Penguin Books is committed to a sustainable
future for our business, our readers and our
planet. This book is made from paper certified
by the Forest Stewardship Council.

Contents

The Foundations of Pleasure   1

On Appetite   3

Elementary Principles   11

The Theory of Frying   66

On Drinks   72

On Gourmandism   77

On the Pleasures of the Table   89

On Restaurateurs   106

Pheasant   118

The Foundations of Pleasure

I. The world is nothing without life, and all that lives takes nourishment.

II. Animals feed: man eats: only the man of intellect knows how to eat.

III. The fate of nations depends on the way they eat.

IV. Tell me what you eat: I will tell you what you are.

V. The Creator, who made man such that he must eat to live, incites him to eat by means of appetite, and rewards him with pleasure.

VI. Gourmandism is an act of judgement, by which we give preference to things which are agreeable to our taste over those which are not.

VII. The pleasures of the table belong to all times and all ages, to every country and every day; they go hand in hand with all our other pleasures, outlast them, and remain to console us for their loss.

VIII. The table is the only place where the first hour is never dull.

IX. The discovery of a new dish does more for the happiness of mankind than the discovery of a star.

X. Drunkards and victims of indigestion do not know how to eat or drink.

XI. The right order of eating is from the most substantial dishes to the lightest.

XII. The right order of drinking is from the mildest wines to the headiest and most perfumed.

XIII. To maintain that one wine may not be drunk after another is heresy; a man's palate can be saturated, and after the third glass the best of wines produces only a dull impression.

XIV. Dessert without cheese is like a pretty woman with only one eye.

XV. A man can become a cook, but he has to be born a *rôtisseur*.

XVI. The most indispensable quality in a cook is punctuality; it is also that of a guest.

XVII. To wait too long for an unpunctual guest is an act of discourtesy towards those who have arrived in time.

XVIII. The man who invites his friends to his table, and fails to give his personal attention to the meal they are going to eat, is unworthy to have any friends.

XIX. The mistress of the house must always see to it that the coffee is excellent, and the master that the liqueurs are of the first quality.

XX. To entertain a guest is to make yourself responsible for his happiness so long as he is beneath your roof.

On Appetite

DEFINITION OF APPETITE

Movement and life are the cause of a continuous wastage of substance in every living body; and the human body, that complicated machine, would soon break down if Providence had not equipped it with a device for warning it when its strength is no longer equal to its needs.

This warning device is appetite. That is the name we give to the first indication of the need for food.

Appetite is heralded by a certain languor in the stomach and a slight feeling of fatigue.

At the same time the brain dwells on objects analogous to its needs; the memory recalls things which have been pleasant to the taste; the imagination pictures them, as it were in a dream. This condition is not without charm; and we have heard thousands of adepts exclaim joyously: 'Oh, what a pleasure it is to have a good appetite, when you know that an excellent meal is waiting for you!'

In the meantime, the whole machinery of nourishment is set in motion: the stomach grows sensitive; the gastric juices rise, the internal gases are noisily displaced; the mouth fills with saliva; and all the digestive powers are up in arms, like soldiers only waiting for the word of command to go into action. A few moments more, and spasmodic movements will begin; there will be yawning, stomach pangs, and finally hunger.

It is possible to observe every phase of these various conditions in any room where people are being kept waiting for dinner.

They are so natural that the most exquisite politeness cannot disguise the symptoms; and hence my aphorism, 'The most indispensable quality in a cook is punctuality.'

ANECDOTE

I shall illustrate this solemn maxim by recalling certain observations I once made at a dinner party, *quorum pars magna fui*, and where the pleasure of observing saved me from the agonies of suffering.

I was invited one day to dinner at the house of an important public official. The invitation was for half past five, and at the proper time everyone had arrived, for it was well known that our host liked his guests to be punctual, and sometimes scolded late-comers.

On arrival I was struck by the air of consternation which reigned among the company; people were whispering into one another's ears and looking out of the window into the courtyard, and some faces wore an expression of stupefaction. Something extraordinary had obviously occurred.

I went up to one of the guests, whom I thought the most likely to be able to satisfy my curiosity, and asked him what was happening. 'Alas,' he replied, in tones of deepest affliction, 'his Grace has been summoned to a

Council of State; he left a moment ago, and who knows when he may be back?' 'Is that all?' I replied, with an air of unconcern which was far from revealing what I really felt. 'Why, that's a matter of a quarter of an hour at the most; some piece of information must be needed which only he can supply; they know that this is an official dinner, and they have no reason to keep us fasting.' So I spoke; but in my heart of hearts I was ill at ease, and I would have preferred to be almost anywhere else.

The first hour went by quickly enough; friends and acquaintances sat down together, exhausted the trivial subjects of conversation, and speculated as to the reason for our good host's summons to the Tuileries.

During the second hour, symptoms of impatience began to appear; anxious glances were exchanged, and the first murmurs of complaint were heard, coming from three or four guests who, having found nowhere to sit down, were not in the best position for waiting.

By the third hour discontent was rife, and everyone was complaining. 'When will he be back?' said one. 'What can he be thinking of?' said another. 'This will be the death of me,' said a third. And every guest kept asking himself the unanswerable question: 'To leave, or not to leave?'

With the fourth hour the symptoms became more pronounced; arms were stretched, to the peril of neighbours' eyes; loud yawns could be heard on all sides; every face was flushed with concentration; and no one listened when I ventured to say that he whose absence was the cause of our misery was doubtless the unhappiest of us all.

Attention was momentarily distracted by an apparition. One of the guests, who was on closer terms with our host than the rest, penetrated as far as the kitchens; he came back breathless and looking as if the end of the world were at hand. Almost inarticulate, in that muffled tone of voice which is a compromise between fear of making a noise and the desire to be heard, he exclaimed: 'His Grace left without giving any instructions, and however long he is away, dinner will not be served before his return.' He spoke; and the consternation caused by his speech will not be surpassed by the effect of the trumpet of the Last Judgement.

Among all these martyrs, the unhappiest was the worthy d'Aigrefeuille, well known to all Paris in those days; his whole body was a mass of suffering, and the anguish of Laocoön was visible on his features. Pale, distracted, seeing nothing, he perched on a chair, folded his little hands across his great belly, and closed his eyes, not to sleep but to wait for death.

But death did not come. About ten o'clock we heard a carriage rolling into the courtyard; everyone stood up spontaneously. Sadness was turned to joy, and five minutes later we were seated at table.

But the time for appetite was past. It was as if we were surprised to find ourselves beginning dinner at such an untimely hour; our jaws failed to work with those isochronous movements which mark an accustomed task, and I later learned that this was a source of some discomfort to several of the guests.

The recommended procedure in such a case is to avoid eating immediately after the hindrance is removed;

a glass of sugared water or a cup of broth should be swallowed first, to soothe the stomach; then an interval of ten or fifteen minutes should elapse, or else the constricted organ will be crushed by the load of food thrust upon it.

LARGE APPETITES

When we read in early literature of the preparations made for the entertainment of two or three persons, and the enormous helpings of food offered to a single guest, it is difficult to avoid the belief that the men who lived nearer than ourselves to the cradle of the world were also endowed with appetites far larger than our own.

Appetites in those days were supposed to increase in proportion to the dignity of the individual; and a man who was served with the entire back of a five-year-old bull would drink from a cup so heavy that he could scarcely lift it.

A few individuals living in more recent times have borne witness to what was done in the past; and historical records are full of examples of almost incredible voracity, applied even to the most repugnant objects.

I will spare my readers these somewhat disgusting details, and instead relate two particular feats of which I myself was a witness, and which call for no blind faith on their part.

About forty years ago I paid a flying visit to the parish priest of Bregnier, a man of great stature, whose appetite was renowned throughout the region.

Although it was barely midday when I arrived, I

found him already seated at table. He had finished the soup and boiled beef, and these two inevitable courses had been followed by a leg of mutton *à la royale*, together with a fine capon and a copious salad.

As soon as I appeared he offered to have a place laid for me, but I declined, and I did well as it turned out; for alone and unaided he briskly put away all there was, namely, the leg of mutton down to the ivory, the capon down to the bone, and the salad down to the bottom of the dish.

A large white cheese was then placed before him, in which he made an angular breach of ninety degrees, washing it down with a bottle of wine and a jug of water; then he took a rest.

What particularly pleased me was that throughout this operation, which lasted about three quarters of an hour, the venerable priest seemed quite unhurried. The huge mouthfuls he tossed into his great maw did not prevent him from laughing and talking; and he devoured everything that had been put before him with no more fuss than if he had been eating a brace of larks.

It was the same with General Bisson, who used to drink eight bottles of wine every morning at breakfast without turning a hair; he had a larger glass than anyone else, and he emptied it more often; but he gave the impression that he did so without thinking, and the business of imbibing two gallons of liquid no more prevented him from joking and issuing his orders than if it had been a glass of water.

General Bisson reminds me of my fellow countryman, the gallant General Prosper Sibuet, who died on the field of honour in 1813 at the passage of the Bober, after serving for many years as chief aide-de-camp to General Masséna.

Prosper was eighteen years old, and the possessor of one of those splendid appetites by which Nature proclaims that she is building up a fine specimen of manhood, when one evening he entered the kitchen of a certain Genin, the host of an inn where the old men of Belley used to meet to eat chestnuts and drink the new white wine of the district, the so-called *vin bourru*.

A magnificent turkey, golden brown, and done to a turn, had just been taken off the spit; the smell of it would have tempted a saint.

The old men, who were no longer hungry, paid little attention to it; but young Prosper's digestive powers were immediately affected. His mouth began to water, and he exclaimed: 'I have only just risen from table, but I'll wager I can eat that fat turkey alone and unaided.'

'*Sez vosu mezé, z'u payo,*' retorted Bouvier du Bouchet, a stout farmer who was present, '*è sez vas caca en rotaz, i-zet vo ket pairé et may ket mezarai la restaz.*'*

The operation began forthwith. The young athlete neatly detached a wing, swallowed it in two mouthfuls, cleaned his teeth by eating the neck of the bird, and drank a glass of wine by way of an interlude.

Next he attacked a leg, ate it as calmly as the wing, and tossed down a second glass of wine to smooth the way for the rest of the fowl.

* 'If you eat it straight off, I'll pay for it, but if you give up on the way, you'll pay, and I'll eat what is left.'

The second wing then followed the first; and the officiant, growing more and more animated, was seizing the last remaining limb, when the unfortunate farmer cried out in dismay:

'*Hai! ze vaie praou qu'izet fotu; m'ez, monche Chibouet, poez kaet zu daive paiet, lessé m'en a m'en mesiet on mocho.*'*

Prosper was as good a fellow then as he afterwards became a good soldier; he granted the request of his antagonist, who was left with the still considerable carcase of the fowl, and paid for both food and drinks with a good grace.

General Sibuet was very fond of relating this feat of youthful prowess; he used to say that he had only granted the farmer's request as a matter of courtesy, and that he felt perfectly capable of winning the wager without this assistance. Certainly what remained of his appetite at the age of forty left no doubt as to the truth of this assertion.

---

* 'Alas! I see that I've lost: but, Monsieur Sibuet, since I've got to pay, at least leave me a morsel to eat.'

I am glad to quote this sample of the dialect of Bugey, in which the *th* of the Greeks and English is used, and, in *praou* and other similar words, a diphthong which exists in no other language, and the sound of which cannot be expressed by any known character. (See the third volume of the *Transactions of the Society of French Antiquaries*.)

Elementary Principles

When I began to write, my list of contents was already drawn up [. . .] but my progress has none the less been slow, because part of my time is devoted to more serious labours.

Meanwhile certain aspects of the subject which I believed to be my private province have been touched on by others; elementary books on chemistry and medicine have been made available to the general public, and doctrines which I expected to be the first to teach have become popular; for example, I had devoted several pages to the chemistry of the *pot-au-feu*, the substance of which is now to be found in several recently published works.

In consequence, I have had to revise that part of my book, reducing it to a few elementary principles, some theories which cannot be repeated too often, and certain observations culled from long experience, which will, I hope, be new to the majority of my readers.

POT-AU-FEU, POTAGE, ETC.

We apply the phrase *pot-au-feu* to a piece of beef boiled in slightly salted water in order to extract its soluble parts.

The liquid which is left at the end of the operation is called *bouillon*.

Finally, the meat from which the soluble part has been extracted is known as *bouilli*.

The water first of all dissolves part of the osmazome; then the albumen, which congeals just below 145 degrees, forming a scum which is usually removed; then the remainder of the osmazome, with the extractive matter of juice; and finally, a few portions of the outer covering of the fibres, which have come away under the continual pressure of the boiling liquid.

To make good *bouillon*, the water has to come to the boil slowly, to prevent the albumen from coagulating inside the meat before extraction; and it should boil almost imperceptibly, so that the various parts which are successively dissolved may be easily and thoroughly united.

Vegetables are added to the *bouillon* to bring out the flavour, and bread or noodles to make it more nutritious; the result is called *potage*.

Potage is a wholesome, light, nutritious food which agrees with everyone; it delights the stomach and stimulates its receptive and digestive faculties. Persons inclined to obesity, however, should take only *bouillon*.

It is generally agreed that nowhere can such good *potage* be obtained as in France; and my own travels have confirmed the truth of this saying. Not that there is anything surprising about that; for *potage* is the basis of the French national diet, and the experience of centuries has inevitably brought it to perfection.

ON *BOUILLI*

The *bouilli* is wholesome food, which rapidly appeases hunger, and is easy enough to digest; but it has little strength in itself, because the meat has lost part of its animalizable juices in the boiling.

As a general rule, it is found that beef which has been boiled has lost half its weight.

Persons who eat *bouilli* may be divided into four categories, as follows:

1. Victims of habit, who eat it because their parents ate it before them, and hope that their children will imitate them with the same implicit obedience;
2. Impatient persons, who detest inactivity at table, and have accordingly contracted the habit of falling upon the first foodstuff that comes to hand (*materiam subjectam*);
3. Careless persons, whom heaven has not blessed with the sacred flame; they regard meals as just part of the day's work, and put all dishes on the same level, sitting at table like oysters on an oyster-bank;
4. Greedy persons, who in an attempt to conceal the extent of their appetites, hastily cast a first victim into their stomach, to appease the devouring gastric fire within and to pave the way for the various consignments they intend to dispatch to the same destination.

Professors never eat *bouilli*, both out of respect for the principles of gastronomy and because they have often preached this undeniable truth to their pupils: '*Bouilli* is meat without its juice.'*

ON POULTRY

I am a great partisan of secondary causes, and devoutly believe that the whole race of fowls was solely created to fill our larders and enrich our banquets.

It is undeniable that from quail to turkey-cock, wherever we meet with a member of this large family, we may be sure of finding food that is both light and savoury, and agrees equally with the convalescent and the man in the best of health; for who among us, after being condemned by a doctor to the diet of a desert father, has not revelled in a nice wing of chicken, the herald of his long-awaited return to social life?

We have not been content, however, with the natural qualities of the gallinaceous species; art has laid hands on them, and under the pretext of improving them, has condemned them to martyrdom. Not only do we take away their means of reproduction, but we keep them in solitary confinement, cast them into darkness, force them to eat willy-nilly, and so blow them up to a size for which they were never intended.

It must be admitted that this unnatural rotundity is also delicious, and that the tender succulence which

---

* This truth is beginning to penetrate, and *bouilli* is no longer served by the self-respecting host; it has been replaced by a roast fillet, a turbot, or a *matelote*.

makes them worthy of our finest tables is due to those reprehensible practices which we have just mentioned.

Thus improved, fowls are to the kitchen what his canvas is to the painter, or to charlatans the cap of Fortunatus; they are served up to us boiled, roasted, fried, hot or cold, whole or in pieces, with or without sauce, boned, skinned, or stuffed, and always with equal success.

Three districts of old-world France dispute the honour of furnishing the best fowls, namely, Caux, Le Mans, and Bresse.

As regards capons there is some doubt as to which is superior, and as a rule the one we are eating seems better than the rest; but as for pullets, there are none to compare with those of Bresse, known as *poulardes fines*; they are round as an apple, and all too rare in Paris, where they never come except in votive hampers.

ON THE TURKEY

The turkey is undoubtedly one of the handsomest presents which the New World has offered to the Old.

Those people who insist on knowing more than anyone else maintain that the Romans were partial to the turkey, that it was served at Charlemagne's wedding-feast, and that it is therefore incorrect to praise the Jesuits for this savoury import.

One could answer these paradoxes with two simple facts:

1. The French name of the bird, *coq d'Inde*, clearly

betrays its origin: for in the old days America was known as the West Indies;

2. The appearance of the bird, which is clearly out-landish.

No scientist could have any doubts on the question.

However, although for my part I was thoroughly convinced, I conducted extensive research into the subject, which I shall spare the reader, and which led me to the following conclusions:

1. That the turkey appeared in Europe towards the end of the seventeenth century;
2. That it was imported by the Jesuits, who bred it in large numbers, especially on one of their farms in the neighbourhood of Bourges;
3. That from there it gradually spread over the whole of France; which is why in many regions the popular word for turkey was and still is *jésuite*;
4. That America is the only place where the turkey has been found wild and in a state of nature (there are none in Africa);
5. That in North America, where it is very common, it is reared either from eggs which are found and hatched out, or from young birds which are caught in the forest and tamed; reared in this way it is nearer to the natural state, and retains its primitive plumage.

Convinced by these points, I would like to observe that we owe a double debt of gratitude to the good Fathers, for they were also responsible for the importation of quinine, which in English is called Jesuit's-bark.

In the course of my researches I also discovered that the acclimatization of the species in France was a gradual process. Enlightened students of the subject have informed me that about the middle of the last century, out of every twenty turkeys hatched, not more than ten grew to maturity; whereas today, all things being equal, the proportion is fifteen in twenty. Rain-storms are particularly fatal to them. The heavy rain-drops, driven by the wind, beat upon their soft, unprotected skulls and kill them.

ON TURKEY-LOVERS

The turkey is the largest of our domestic fowls, and if not the most delicately flavoured at least the most savoury.

It has also the unique merit of attracting all classes of society.

When the vine-grower or the ploughman wants a treat on some long winter evening, what do we see roasting over a bright fire in the kitchen where the table is laid? A turkey.

When the hard-working artisan invites a few friends to his house to enjoy a holiday which is all the more precious for being rare, what is sure to be the principal dish of the feast? A turkey, stuffed with sausages or Lyons chestnuts.

And in the high places of gastronomy, at those select gatherings where politics are forced to give way to dissertations upon taste, what do the guests hope for and long for as the second course? A truffled turkey! . . . And my secret memoirs contain a note to the effect that its potent juices have often brought a glow to eminently diplomatic features.

INFLUENCE OF THE TURKEY
ON FINANCE

The importation of turkeys has produced a considerable accretion to the public purse, and given rise to an important trade.

By rearing turkeys, the farmer can pay his rent more easily, and his daughters can often save up enough for their dowries; for city dwellers must pay well if they wish to feast on that foreign flesh.

The financial importance of the truffled turkey deserves special mention.

I have reason to believe that from the beginning of November to the end of February three hundred truffled turkeys are consumed in Paris every day, or thirty-six thousand in the whole period.

The ordinary price of a turkey so prepared is at least 20 francs, which gives a total of 720,000 francs – a tidy sum to be in circulation. To this must be added an equivalent sum for chickens, pheasants, and partridges, likewise truffled, which are displayed every day in the food shops, to the agony of those beholders who cannot afford to buy them.

AN EXPLOIT OF THE PROFESSOR

During my stay at Hartford, in Connecticut, I had the good fortune to shoot a wild turkey. Such an exploit is worthy to be handed down to posterity, and I shall recount it all the more readily in that I am the hero of the tale.

A worthy old American farmer, who lived in the back-woods, had asked me to join him for a few days' shooting, promising me partridges, grey squirrels, and wild turkeys, and inviting me to bring along a friend or two.

Accordingly, one fine day in October 1794, Mr King and I set out on a couple of hired hacks, in the hope of arriving by nightfall at Mr Bulow's farm, situated five mortal leagues from Hartford, Connecticut.

Mr King was a peculiar sort of sportsman; he was passionately fond of shooting; but whenever he killed a bird he used to curse himself as a murderer and give vent to elegies and moral reflections on the fate of the victim; after which he would repeat the offence.

Although the road was little more than a rough track, we reached our destination without mishap, and were welcomed with that quiet but cordial hospitality which is expressed in deeds rather than words; that is to say, in a few moments suitable greetings had been extended to us and comforts provided for men, horses, and dogs.

We devoted about two hours to an inspection of the farm and its outbuildings; I could describe it all if I wished, but I prefer to introduce my readers to Mr Bulow's four buxom daughters, for whom our arrival was a great event.

Their ages ranged from sixteen to twenty; they were radiant with freshness and health, and there was a simplicity and natural grace about them which lent a thousand charms to their most ordinary actions.

Shortly after our return from the tour of inspection, we sat down to a copious meal. There was a superb piece of corned beef, a stewed goose, a magnificent leg of mutton, a vast selection of vegetables, and at either end of the table two huge jugs of a cider so excellent that I could have gone on drinking it for ever.

When we had shown our host that we were true sportsmen, at least as far as appetite was concerned, he turned to the object of our visit; he indicated to us as best he could the places where we might expect to find game, the landmarks which would guide us on our way back, and above all the farms where we could obtain refreshment.

During this conversation the young ladies had made some excellent tea, of which we drank several cups; after which we were shown to a room with two beds, where we soon fell asleep under the influence of exercise and good cheer.

The next day we set out rather late in the morning, and, once past the limit of Mr Bulow's clearings, I found myself for the first time in virgin forest, where the sound of an axe had never been heard.

I walked along in delight, observing the benefits and ravages of time the creator and destroyer, and following with interest the successive phases in the life of an oak, from the moment when it emerges from the soil with a couple of leaves to the time when nothing is left of it but a long dark stain, the dust of its heart.

Mr King, however, scolded me for my daydreaming, and we set about our sport. Our first victims were a few of those pretty little grey partridges which are so plump and tender. Then we brought down six or seven grey squirrels, which are highly prized in those parts; and finally our lucky star brought us into the middle of a flock of turkeys.

They flew off at short intervals one after another, flapping their wings noisily, and screaming raucously. Mr King fired first and ran after his bird; the rest all appeared to be out of range, but then a straggler rose, not ten paces from where I stood; I fired at him above a clearing, and he fell stone-dead.

Only a sportsman can understand the joy I felt at that perfect shot. I took that glorious bird and had been turning him this way and that for a full quarter of an hour when I heard Mr King calling for help. I ran to join him, and found that he only wanted me to help him in the search for a turkey which he swore that he had shot, but which had none the less disappeared completely.

I put my dog on the trail, but he led us into some undergrowth which was so dense and prickly that it would have stopped a snake, and we were forced to abandon the search; this put my companion into a bad temper which lasted until he reached home.

The remainder of our day's sport was not worth recording. Going home, we lost our way in those boundless woods, and we were resigning ourselves to a night in the open, when we heard the silvery voices of our hostesses and the deep bass of their papa; they had been kind enough to come to meet us, and our troubles were over.

The four sisters were ready for us: best dresses, new sashes, pretty bonnets, and dainty shoes showed that they had gone out of their way to please; and for my part, when one of them came up to me and took my arm, for all the world as if she were my wife, I resolved to show her every courtesy.

When we reached the farm we found supper waiting

for us; but before tackling it, we sat down for a moment in front of a blazing fire which had been lit for us, despite the mildness of the weather. We felt a lot better for it, and our tiredness vanished as if by magic.

This practice had no doubt been borrowed from the Indians, who always keep a fire burning in their tents. Or perhaps it has come down to us from Saint Francis of Sales, who said that a fire was a good thing for twelve months in the year. (*Non liquet*).

We ate like starving men; a generous bowl of punch helped us to round off the evening, and our conversation, to which our host contributed more freely than the previous day, lasted far into the night.

We spoke of the War of Independence, in which Mr Bulow had served as a senior officer; of Monsieur de la Fayette, whose memory grows ever dearer in the hearts of all Americans, who never speak of him but by his title, as the Marquis; of agriculture, which at that time was bringing great prosperity to the United States; and lastly of our own dear France, which I loved more than ever since I had been forced to leave her shores.

By way of an interlude, Mr Bulow would turn now and then to his eldest daughter and say, 'Maria, give us a song.' She never needed to be asked a second time, but with a charming air of embarrassment sang the national tune of 'Yankee Doodle', 'Queen Mary's Elegy', and 'Major André's Lament', all popular songs in that country. Maria had taken a few lessons, and in those remote parts passed for something of a *virtuosa*; but the chief merit of her singing lay in the quality of her voice, which was soft, unaffected, and clear.

Next morning we took our leave, despite our host's friendly insistence that we should stay. While the horses were being saddled, Mr Bulow took me to one side, and spoke the following remarkable words:

'If there is a happy man under heaven, my dear sir, you see that man in me; everything around you, and everything you have seen in my house, comes from my own property. These stockings were knitted by my daughters; my shoes and clothing came from my animals, and they together with my garden and my poultry-yard provide me with my plain but ample fare; and, which is greatly to the credit of our Government, Connecticut contains thousands of farmers as happily placed as I am, and whose doors, like mine, are never locked.

'The taxes here are almost nothing, and so long as they are paid we can sleep in peace. Congress does everything in its power to help our budding industry; agents travel the country in every direction to purchase what we have to sell; and I have now enough money for a long time to come, for I have just been paid twenty-four dollars a ton for flour which I usually give away at eight.

'All this comes from the liberty which we have won by force of arms and based on good laws. I am my own master, and you will not be surprised to learn that the sound of the drum is never heard here, and that except on the Fourth of July, the glorious anniversary of our independence, neither soldiers, uniforms, nor bayonets are ever to be seen.'

During the whole of our homeward journey I was absorbed in deep reflection; it will perhaps be thought that my mind was full of Mr Bulow's parting words, but in fact the subject of my thoughts was quite different; I was thinking of how I would cook my turkey, and I was worried by the fear that Hartford would be unable to furnish all my needs; for I wished to make my mark by using my spoils to the best possible advantage.

I am making a painful sacrifice in omitting the details of the trouble I took to prepare a distinguished meal for the American guests I had invited. It must suffice to say that the partridge wings were served *en papillote* and the grey squirrels stewed in Madeira.

As for the turkey, which was our only roast dish, it was charming to behold, pleasing to smell, and delicious to taste. And so, until the last morsel was consumed, from all round the table came cries of 'Very good!' 'Exceedingly good!' 'My dear sir, what a glorious dish!'*

ON GAME

The term *game* includes all animals which live in a state of natural liberty in fields and woods, and which are fit to be eaten.

---

* The flesh of the wild turkey has more colour and flavour than that of the domestic variety.

It gave me great pleasure to learn that my esteemed colleague, Monsieur Bosc, had shot turkeys in Carolina, and that he had found them excellent, and far superior to those we rear in Europe. He accordingly advises breeders to allow the birds as much liberty as possible, letting them range the fields and even the woods, in order to enhance their flavour and bring them to their original condition. (*Annales d'Agriculture*, 28 February 1821.)

We say 'fit to be eaten', because some animals do not come under the category of game. Such are foxes, badgers, crows, magpies, owls, etc., which we call *vermin*.

Game is divided into three classes:

The first begins with the thrush, and includes, in a descending scale, all the lesser birds.

The second begins with the corncrake and includes the woodcock, the partridge, the pheasant, the rabbit, and the hare; this is game in the proper sense of the term – ground game and marsh game, furry game and feathered game.

The third is more generally known by the name of venison, and comprises the wild boar, the roe deer, and all the other hoofed animals.

Game is one of our favourite foods, being wholesome, tasty, full-flavoured, and easily digestible by all except the aged.

But these qualities are not so inherent as to be independent of the cook's skill. Throw a pinch of salt, some water, and a piece of beef into the pot, and you will obtain *potage* and *boulli*. Repeat the process, but with wild boar or deer instead of the beef, and you will be disappointed by the result; in this instance, the advantage lies with the butcher's meat.

But in the hands of a skilled cook, game undergoes a great many modifications and transformations, and provides most of the full-flavoured dishes which constitute transcendental cookery.

A great part of the merit of game is due to the nature of its breeding-ground; the taste of a red Périgord partridge is not the same as that of a red partridge from

Sologne; and while a hare shot in the plains around Paris makes only a mediocre dish, a leveret born in the parched highlands of Valromey or Upper Dauphiné is perhaps the most savoury of all quadrupeds.

Among the small birds, the first in order of excellence is beyond question the warbler.

It grows at least as fat as the robin or the ortolan, and Nature has further endowed it with a unique flavour of such exquisite bitterness that it stimulates, satisfies, and delights the organ of taste. If the warbler were as large as a pheasant, it would easily command the price of an acre of land.

It is a great pity that this privileged bird is such a rarity in Paris; it is true that a few are to be found in the capital, but they lack that plumpness which is their whole merit, and can scarcely be said to bear any resemblance to those of the eastern or southern regions of France.*

Few people know how to eat a small bird; here is the method, as it was privately revealed to me by Canon Charcot, a born gourmand, who was a perfect gastronome some thirty years before the word was invented.

---

* In my youth tales were still told at Belley of the Jesuit Father Fabi, a native of that diocese, and his passion for warblers.

No sooner did the hawkers start selling them in the streets than people said: 'Here are the warblers! Father Fabi must be on his way!' Sure enough, he never failed to arrive on the first of September with a friend; they came to feast on warblers as long as the season lasted; everyone in the region made a point of inviting them to a meal, and they left about the twenty-fifth.

So long as he was in France, he never missed his annual

26

Take a plump little bird by the beak, sprinkle him with a little salt, remove the gizzard, thrust him boldly into your mouth, bite him off close to your fingers, and chew hard; this will produce enough juice to wet the whole organ, and you will taste a delight unknown to the common herd:

Odi profanum vulgus et arceo.* (Horace)

Among game properly so called, the quail is the daintiest and most delightful. A plump quail is equally appealing in taste, shape, and colour. It is an admission of ignorance to serve it up otherwise than roasted or *en papillote*, because its flavour is extremely ephemeral, and, if the animal comes into contact with any liquid, it dissolves, evaporates, and is lost.

The woodcock is another very distinguished bird; but few people are aware of all its charms. A woodcock is never in all its glory except when roasted under the eye of a sportsman, and preferably the sportsman who killed it; then the dish is prepared in accordance with the rules, and the mouth grows moist in the anticipation of delight.

But over all these birds, and all others too, the pheasant takes precedence; yet few mortals know how to present it to perfection.

---

ornithophilical excursions, which only came to an end when he was in Rome, where he died in the office of Penitentiary in 1688.

Father Fabi (Honoré) was a man of great learning; he published various works on theology and physics, in one of which he sought to prove that he had discovered the circulation of the blood before or at least as early as Harvey.

* 'I hate the ignorant crowd and keep it off.' [Ed.]

A pheasant eaten within a week of its death is not as grand as a partridge or a chicken, for its whole merit lies in its aroma.

Science has investigated the expansion of that aroma, experiment has turned theory into practice, and a pheasant cooked at the right moment is a dish worthy of the most exalted gourmands.

The reader will find in the *Miscellanea* a description of the manner of roasting pheasants called *à la Sainte Alliance*. The time has come for this method, hitherto confined to a small circle of friends, to be made known far and wide for the happiness of mankind. A truffled pheasant is not as good as might be imagined; the bird has too little moisture to anoint the tuber; and moreover, the flavour of the one and the fragrance of the other neutralize each other, or rather are incompatible.

ON FISH

Certain sages, of somewhat unorthodox tendencies, maintain that the Ocean was the common cradle of all existing things; that the human race itself was born in the sea; and that it owes its present condition only to the influence of the air and the habits it has been forced to acquire in order to live in this unfamiliar element.

Be that as it may, it is at least certain that the watery realm contains a vast number of creatures of all shapes and sizes, endowed with vital properties in widely differing proportions, on a system totally unlike that which governs the warm-blooded animals.

It is also certain that at all times and in all parts of the world, it furnishes a vast quantity of foodstuffs, and that, in the present state of science, it provides our tables with a most agreeable variety of dishes.

Fish, being less nutritious than flesh and more succulent than vegetables, is a *mezzo termine* which suits almost every temperament, and may be allowed even to convalescents.

The Greeks and Romans, though less advanced than ourselves in the art of seasoning fish, nevertheless prized it highly, and carried delicacy to the point of being able to tell by the taste in which waters their fish had been caught.

They kept fish alive in tanks; and the reader will doubtless know of the cruel practice of Vadius Pollo, who killed his slaves to feed their corpses to his eels: a practice of which the Emperor Domitian strongly disapproved, although he regrettably failed to punish the offender.

There has been a great deal of argument about the rival merits of sea fish and freshwater fish.

The question will probably never be decided for as the Spanish proverb says, *sobre los gustos, no hai disputa.** Everyone is affected after his own manner; such sensations are too ephemeral to be expressed by any known character, and there is no scale to determine whether a cod, a sole, or a turbot is superior to a salmon trout, a fine pike, or even a six- or seven-pound tench.

It is certain, however, that fish is much less nourishing than meat, either because it contains no osmazome,

---

* 'One can't argue about tastes.' [Ed.]

or because, being much lighter in weight, it contains less matter in the same volume. Shell-fish, and especially oysters, provide little nourishing substance; and this is the reason why so many can be eaten immediately before a meal without any harmful effects.

In the old days, a meal of any note usually began with oysters, and there were always a good many guests who did not stop before they had swallowed a gross (twelve dozen, a hundred and forty-four). Wishing to know the weight of this advance-guard, I investigated the matter, and found that a dozen oysters, water included, weighed four ounces, and a gross, therefore, three pounds. Now, I am convinced that the same individuals, who were not prevented by the oysters from eating a copious meal, would have been completely sated if they had eaten a like quantity of meat, even if it had only been chicken.

Anecdote

In 1798 I was at Versailles as a commissioner of the Directory, and had fairly frequent dealings with Monsieur Laperte, who was secretary to the tribunal of the department; he was extremely fond of oysters, and used to complain of never having eaten enough of them, or, as he put it, 'had his bellyful of them'.

I decided to provide him with that satisfaction, and to that end invited him to dinner.

He came; I kept him company as far as the third dozen, after which I let him go on alone. He went up to thirty-two dozen, taking more than an hour over the task, for the servant was not very skilful at opening them.

Meanwhile, I was inactive, and as that is a distressing

condition to be in at the table, I stopped my guest when he was still in full career. 'My dear fellow,' I said, 'it is not your fate to eat your bellyful of oysters today; let us have dinner.'

We dined: and he acquitted himself with the vigour and appetite of a man who had been fasting.

MURIA AND GARUM

The ancients extracted two very choice sauces from fish, namely *muria* and *garum*.

The first was simply brine of tunny-fish, or to be more precise, the liquid substance drawn from that fish by the addition of salt.

About *garum*, which was costlier, much less is known to us today. It is said to have been obtained by pressure from the soused entrails of mackerel or scomber; but if this were so, there would be no reason for its high price. There are some grounds for believing that it was a foreign sauce, and it may have been nothing more than *soy*, which we import from India, and which is known to be an extract from fish fermented with mushrooms.

Certain races are reduced by their geographical position to living almost entirely on fish; they also give it to their draught animals, which are eventually inured by habit to this strange diet, and even use it as manure for their fields; yet the surrounding sea never fails to supply them with the same quantity.

It has been remarked that these peoples are less courageous than the flesh-eating races; they are pale in complexion, which is not at all surprising, because the component elements of fish are such as to augment the lymph rather than to strengthen the blood.

Many instances of longevity have also been observed among the ichthyophagous nations; either because their relatively light and unsubstantial diet saves them from the evils of plethora, or because the juices of fish, being designed by Nature solely for the formation of fish-bone and gristle destined to last a very short time, have the effect on human beings of retarding the solidification of all parts of the body which finally becomes the inevitable cause of natural death.

Be that as it may, fish, in the hands of a skilful cook, can become an inexhaustible source of gustatory delight; whether it is served up whole, chopped up, or in slices, boiled, fried in oil, cooked in wine, hot or cold, it is always well received; but it is never more welcome than when it appears in the form of a *matelote*.

Although this stew is imposed by necessity upon our bargees, and is only brought to perfection in riverside taverns, it is neverthless invested by them with unsurpassable virtues; and ichthyophiles never see it without going into raptures, some praising its wholesome taste, some its combination of several qualities, and others because it is possible to go on eating it almost indefinitely without fear of satiety or indigestion.

Analytical chemistry has been used to investigate the effects of a fish diet on the animal economy, and the results all go to show that it has a powerful effect on the sense of physical desire, and arouses the instinct of reproduction in both sexes.

Once the effect had been established, two immediate

causes were ascertained, which anyone could appreciate, namely:

1. Certain ways of preparing fish, with seasoning of an obviously stimulating nature, such as caviare, red herring, soused tunny-fish, cod, stock-fish, and others;
2. The different juices contained in fish, which are highly inflammable and become oxygenated and rancid on digestion.

Closer analysis has revealed a third and even more potent cause, namely the presence of phosphorus, which is to be found already formed in the milt, and never fails to appear on decomposition.

These physical truths were doubtless unknown to the ecclesiastical authorities who imposed the quadragesimal fast on various religious communities, such as the Carthusians, the Recollects, the Trappists, and the Barefoot Carmelites of the reformed order of Saint Theresa; for it cannot be supposed that they wished to make the vow of chastity, which was already anti-social enough, even more difficult to keep.

No doubt under those conditions splendid victories were won, and rebellious senses quelled; but what falls occurred too, and what defeats! Tales of those defeats must have had a foundation in fact to invest a religious order with a reputation like that of Hercules among the daughters of Danaus, or Marshal de Saxe with Mademoiselle Lecouvreur.

For that matter, they might have found enlightenment in a tale which was already old in their day, since it has come down to us from the Crusades.

Sultan Saladin, wishing to find out to what lengths the dervishes could carry their continence, confined two within his palace, and for a given time had them fed on the most succulent meats.

Soon all trace of the severities they had practised on themselves was lost, and their bellies began to fill out again.

At this point two odalisques of surpassing beauty were given to them to be their companions; but their most skilful wiles failed to achieve their object, and the two saints emerged from this testing ordeal as pure as the diamond of Vizapoor.

The Sultan kept them in his palace, and to celebrate their triumph had them fed on a diet no less succulent than before, but consisting exclusively of fish.

After a few weeks they were exposed again to the twin powers of youth and beauty; but this time Nature prevailed, and the happy cenobites succumbed . . . magnificently.

In the present state of our knowledge it is probable that, if the course of events brought some monastic order back into being, the superiors in charge of the monks would adopt a diet more favourable to the accomplishment of their duties.

PHILOSOPHICAL REFLECTION

Fish, taken collectively in all their species, offer the philosopher an endless source of meditation and surprise.

The various forms of these strange creatures, the senses which they lack, the limited powers of those which they possess, the influence on their habits of the element in which they live and breathe and move, all combine to extend the range of our ideas, and our understanding of the infinite modifications which may arise from matter, movement, and life.

For my part, I look upon them with a feeling akin to respect, born of the conviction that they are antediluvian creatures; for the vast cataclysm which drowned our great-uncles about eight hundred years after the creation of the world was a time of joy, conquest, and festivity for the fishes.

ON TRUFFLES

Whoever says 'truffles' utters a great word which arouses erotic and gastronomic memories among the skirted sex, and memories gastronomic and erotic among the bearded sex.

This dual distinction is due to the fact that the noble tuber is not only considered delicious to the taste, but is also believed to foster powers the exercise of which is extremely pleasurable.

The origin of the truffle is unknown; it is found, but nobody knows anything of its birth or growth. The greatest minds have pondered over it; at one time it was thought that its seed had been discovered, and it was declared that truffles might be sown at will. Vain efforts and illusory promises! No harvest was ever reaped from that sowing; and perhaps that is no great misfortune; for since the price of truffles is partly a matter of caprice, they might well be held in less esteem if they were available in quantity and cheap.

'Rejoice, my dear,' I said one day to Madame de V—; 'a loom has just been shown to the Society for Encouragement on which it will be possible to manufacture superb lace for practically nothing.'

'Why,' the lady replied, with an air of supreme indifference, 'if lace were cheap, do you think anybody would want to wear such rubbish?'

EROTIC PROPERTY OF TRUFFLES

Truffles were known to the Romans; but it does not appear that they ever tasted the French variety. Those which they enjoyed came from Greece, Africa, and above all Libya; their substance was white and reddish, and the Libyan truffles were the most sought after, as being at once more tender and more fragrant.

*Gustus elementa per omnia quaerunt.** (Juvenal)

After the Romans a long interval occurred, and it was only recently that the truffle was rediscovered, for I have read several old cookery books in which no mention is made of it; its rediscovery may be said to have been witnessed by the generation which is passing away as I write.

About 1780, truffles were a rarity in Paris, being only obtainable, and then just in small quantities, at the Hôtel des Américains and the Hôtel de Provence; and a truffled turkey was a great luxury, only to be seen on the tables of great lords or courtesans.

* 'They ransack all the elements for delicacies.' [Ed.]

We owe the increased supplies of the present day to the provision merchants, whose numbers have grown considerably, and who, seeing that truffles were finding favour, sent agents all over the kingdom. By paying good prices and using mail couriers and stage-coaches as means of transport, these agents made truffle-hunting a general activity; for since truffles cannot be planted, it is only by diligent searching that consumption can be increased.

It is safe to say that at the time of writing (1825), the fame of the truffle is at its zenith. Nobody dares to admit having been present at a meal which did not include a single truffled dish. However good in itself an entrée may be, it makes a poor show if it is not garnished with truffles. Who has not felt his mouth water at the very mention of truffles *à la provençale*?

A *sauté* of truffles is a dish of which the mistress of the house always does the honours herself; in short, the truffle is the jewel of cookery.

I set out to find the reason for this preference, for it seemed to me that several other substances had an equal claim to the honour; and I found that reason in the widespread belief that truffles are conducive to erotic pleasure; what is more, I became convinced that nearly all our tastes, predilections, and admirations are born of the same cause, so closely are we held in thrall by that most capricious and tyrannical of the senses.

The discovery prompted me to try to find out whether the popular belief was well founded and the property attributed to truffles a reality. An investigation of this sort is no doubt somewhat indelicate and likely to provoke cynical laughter. But *honni soit qui mal y pense*: the pursuit of truth is always praiseworthy.

I first of all approached the ladies, on account of their keen perception and sense of tact, but it was soon borne in on me that I should have embarked on my inquiries forty years earlier, for all the replies I received were ironical or evasive. Only one lady was frank with me, and I propose to quote here what she told me; she is a woman who is witty but unpretentious, virtuous but no prude, and for whom love is now only a pleasant memory.

'Monsieur,' she said to me, 'one day long ago when suppers were still the fashion, I supped at home *en trio* with my husband and a friend of his. Verseuil (that was the name of this friend) was a handsome fellow, not without wit, and a frequent visitor to my house; but he had never said anything to me to make me look on him in the light of a prospective lover, and if he occasionally paid me compliments, they were so discreet that only a fool could have taken offence at them. On the day in question he seemed destined to keep me company for the rest of the evening, for my husband had a business appointment and was due to leave us before long. The basis of our supper, which was a light meal, was a superb truffled fowl which the sub-delegate from Périgueux had sent us. In those days such a dish was a great luxury, and you can guess from its origin that in this case it was perfection itself. The truffles in particular were delicious, and you know how I love them. All the same, I restrained myself, and what is more, I drank only one glass of champagne; I had some sort of womanly premonition that something would happen before the evening was out.

38

'After a while my husband went off, leaving me alone with Verseuil, whom he regarded as completely harmless. At first we talked of matters of no consequence, but soon the conversation took a much narrower and more interesting turn. Verseuil was first complimentary, then expansive, affectionate, and tender, and finally, when he saw that I was simply amused by all his sweet nothings, so importunate that I could no longer have any doubts about his intentions. At that point I awoke as from a dream, and defended myself all the more sincerely in that my heart said nothing to me in his favour. He persisted, with an ardour which seemed likely to become dangerous; I was hard put to it to keep him at arm's length, and I admit to my shame that I only succeeded in doing so by persuading him that all hope was not denied to him in the future. Finally he took his leave; I went to bed and slept like a log. But the next day was the day of judgement; I examined my conduct of the previous evening, and found it reprehensible. I ought to have stopped Verseuil at his first words and not lent myself to a conversation which boded no good. My pride ought to have been aroused earlier, and my eyes armed with severity; I should have rung the bell, screamed, flown into a rage, in a word done everything I failed to do. What shall I say, Monsieur? I put it all down to the truffles; I am genuinely convinced that they had given me a dangerous predisposition; and if I have not abstained from them since (that would have been too drastic a step), at least I never eat them now without any pleasure they afford me being mingled with a little mistrust.'

A confession, however frank it may be, can never

carry the weight of a doctrine. I therefore looked for further information; I searched my memory and consulted those men who by their profession are invested with special trust. I gathered them together in a committee, court, senate, sanhedrin, and areopagus; and we arrived at the following conclusion, which I offer for comment to the writers of the twenty-fifth century:

'The truffle is not a true aphrodisiac; but in certain circumstances it can make women more affectionate and men more attentive.'

White truffles are found in Piedmont which are highly esteemed; they have a faint taste of garlic, which does not mar their perfection in the slightest, because it has no unpleasant after-effects.

The best truffles in France come from Périgord and Upper Provence; they attain their full flavour about the month of January.

Those which come from Bugey are also very choice; but this kind has the defect of being difficult to preserve. I myself have made four attempts, for the benefit of those who stroll on the banks of the Seine, and only one was successful; but at least on that occasion my guests recognized both the goodness of the thing and the merits of difficulty overcome.

Burgundy and Dauphiné truffles are of poor quality; they are hard and lack substance; thus there are truffles and truffles, just as there are degrees of merit in everything else.

In order to find truffles, recourse is usually had to dogs and pigs trained for the purpose; but there are also men with so practised an eye that they have only to look at a field to be able to say with some certainty whether it contains truffles, and if so, what their size and quality will be.

Are Truffles Indigestible?

It only remains for us to discover whether the truffle is indigestible.

Our answer will be in the negative.

This official and final decision is founded:

1. On the nature of the actual subject of our inquiry (the truffle is easy to masticate, weighs very little, and is neither hard nor tough);
2. On our own observations, conducted over more than fifty years, in the course of which we have never seen a single truffle-eater suffering from indigestion;
3. On the evidence of the most famous practitioners in Paris, which is a city of gourmands, and eminently trufflivorous;
4. And lastly, on the daily conduct of the legal fraternity, who, all things being equal, consume more truffles than any other class of citizens; witness, among others, Doctor Malouet, who used to eat enough of them to give an elephant indigestion, but who nevertheless lived to the age of eighty-six.

Hence it may be taken for certain that the truffle is a food as wholesome as it is agreeable, and that, eaten in moderation, it goes down as easily as a letter into a postbox.

That is not to say that indisposition may not be felt after a copious meal at which, among other things, truffles have been eaten; but such accidents only befall persons who after stuffing themselves at the first course, cram even more food into their mouths at the second, in their anxiety to miss none of the good things placed before them.

Then their indigestion is not the fault of the truffles; and it is certain that they would have suffered even greater agonies if instead of truffles they had in similar circumstances eaten the same quantity of potatoes.

Let us conclude with a true story, which shows how easily a mistake can arise from imperfect observation.

One day I had invited Monsieur S— to dine with me, a charming old gentleman, and a gourmand of the first rank. Either because I did not know his tastes, or in order to prove to all my guests that I had their happiness at heart, I had not been sparing with the truffles, which appeared under the aegis of a virgin turkey stuffed to advantage.

Monsieur S— fell upon them avidly, and as I knew that he had not died of them so far, I let him be, begging him not to go too fast, for no one had designs on his property.

All went well, and it was quite late when he took his leave; but on reaching home he was seized with violent stomach-ache, accompanied by retching, coughing and general sickness.

This disquieting state of affairs continued for some time: and had already been diagnosed as indigestion due to truffles, when Nature suddenly came to the patient's rescue. Monsieur S— opened his mouth wide, and shot out a single fragment of truffle, which hit the wall and rebounded with enough force to imperil the people attending to him.

All the distressing symptoms promptly ceased; calm

was restored; the patient's digestion resumed its normal course, and he fell asleep to wake next morning in good fettle and completely unembittered by his experience.

The cause of the trouble was soon discovered. Monsieur S— has been eating for a great many years, and his teeth have proved unable to cope with the task he has imposed on them; some of the precious ivories have emigrated, and the rest no longer coincide as well as could be wished.

Under these conditions, one truffle had escaped mastication and gone down nearly whole; the action of digestion had carried it towards the pylorus, where it had temporarily lodged; this lodgement had been the cause of the evil, even as the expulsion of the truffle was the remedy.

Thus there was no indigestion, but only a blockage caused by the presence of a foreign body.

Such was the decision reached by the examining committee who saw the evidence and graciously invited me to report their findings.

Monsieur S— has none the less remained as fervently devoted to the truffle as ever, and still attacks it with all his old audacity; but he is careful to masticate it more thoroughly and swallow it more carefully; and he thanks God in the joy of his heart for enabling this sanitary precaution to prolong his earthly pleasures.

ON SUGAR

In our present state of scientific knowledge, we understand sugar to mean a sweet-tasting crystallizable substance, resoluble by fermentation into carbonic acid and alcohol.

Formerly the word implied the solidified and crystallized juice of the sugar-cane (*arundo saccharifera*).

This reed was originally found in the Indies; and it is certain that the Romans had no knowledge of sugar, either as a common article of food or as a crystal.

There are, it is true, a few pages in ancient literature which seem to indicate knowledge of the art of extracting a sweet substance from certain reeds: Lucan says:

Quique bibunt tenera dulces ab arundine succos.*

But there is a considerable difference between water sweetened by a substance extracted from cane and sugar as we now know it; and the art had reached only a rudimentary stage among the Romans.

It was in the colonies of the New World that sugar really originated; the cane was imported there about two centuries ago, and flourished. Attempts were made to use its sweet juices, and after a series of experiments syrup, crude sugar, molasses, and refined sugar were successively extracted from them.

The cultivation of the sugar-cane has become an affair of prime importance; for it is a source of wealth not only to those who grow it, but also to those who process it, those who trade in its products, and those governments which tax it.

On Indigenous Sugar

For a long time it was believed that tropical heat was essential for the production of sugar, but about 1740

* 'And who drink the sweet juice from the tender reed.' [Ed.]

44

Margraff discovered its presence in certain plants in the temperate zone, including beetroot: and his discovery was confirmed by Professor Achard's experiments in Berlin.

At the beginning of the nineteenth century, when circumstances had made sugar scarce, and consequently dear in France, the Government appealed to scientists to make it an object of research.

This appeal was highly successful, and it was found that sugar was widely present in the vegetable kingdom; it was discovered in the grape, the chestnut, the potato, and above all the beetroot.

This last plant was made the object of widespread cultivation, and a host of experiments took place which showed that in this respect the Old World could dispense with the services of the New. Factories sprang up all over France and met with varying degrees of success; the new art of saccharinification was naturalized, and the day may come when circumstances will force us to revive it.

The most important of these factories was the one which Monsieur Benjamin Delessert, a worthy citizen whose name is always associated with what is useful and good, established at Passy, near Paris.

A series of extensive operations enabled him to rid the process of its dubious elements; he made no secret of his discoveries, even to those who might have been tempted to become his rivals; the head of the Government visited him in person, and appointed him purveyor to the palace of the Tuileries.

When new circumstances, the Restoration and peace, brought back cheap sugar from the colonies, the beet-sugar factories lost a great part of their advantages. But several of them still flourish, and Monsieur Benjamin Delessert makes huge quantities every year at a fair profit, thus preserving methods which may well prove useful in the future.*

When beet sugar was first put on the market, prejudiced persons and ignorant masses declared that it tasted unpleasant and was inefficient as a sweetener; some even maintained that it was unwholesome.

The contrary has been proved by a series of exact experiments; and Monsieur le Comte Chaptal has embodied the result of these in his excellent work, *Chemistry Applied to Agriculture*, first edition, volume ii, page 12.

'The sugars extracted from these various plants,' says the famous chemist, 'are of exactly the same nature, and differ in no respect from one another, when they have been refined to the same degree of purity. Taste, crystallization, colour, and specific gravity are absolutely identical, and the most experienced judge or consumer of these products may be defied to tell one from another.'

A striking example of the force of prejudice and the difficulty of establishing the truth is to be observed in

---

* It may be added that the Society for the Encouragement of National Industry, at its general meeting, awarded a gold medal to Monsieur Crespel of Arras, who every year manufactures more than one hundred and fifty thousand pieces of beet sugar; and is able to make a profitable living, even when the price of cane sugar falls as low as 2 fr. 20 c. the kilogramme; this is because he has succeeded in utilizing the residue, from which he extracts spirits by distillation and which he then uses as cattle-fodder.

Great Britain, where not ten persons in a hundred, chosen at random, believe that it is possible to make sugar out of beetroot.

Different Uses of Sugar

Sugar entered the world by way of the apothecary's laboratory. The importance of the part it proceeded to play in that laboratory may be judged from the old saying about anyone who lacked something essential, that he was 'like an apothecary without sugar'.

The fact that it came from such a source was enough to ensure that it obtained an unfavourable reception; some said that it heated the blood, some that it attacked the lungs, others that it was a cause of apoplexy; but calumny was forced to give way to truth, and more than eighty years have passed since someone coined that memorable aphorism: 'Sugar harms nothing but the purse.'

Under such an impenetrable aegis, sugar came every day into more general use, and there is no alimentary substance which has undergone more amalgamations and transformations.

Many people like eating pure sugar, and in some cases, most of them desperate, the doctors prescribe it in that form, as a remedy which can do no harm, and is at least pleasant to take.

Mixed with water, it is a refreshing, wholesome, and agreeable drink, which is sometimes effective as a medicine.

Mixed with a small proportion of water and subjected to heat, it produces syrups, to which any kind of flavour may be added; these drinks are always refreshing, and are so varied that they please every taste.

Mixed with water from which the calorie is then extracted it produces ices, which originated in Italy, and seem to have been introduced into France by Catherine de Médicis.

Mixed with wine, it produces a cordial, with such well-known restorative qualities that in some countries it is poured over cakes which are brought to newly married couples on their wedding night; just as in Persia the bride and groom are given sheep's trotters in vinegar.

Mixed with flour and eggs, it produces biscuits, macaroons, cracknels, sponge cakes, and all the many kinds of light pastry which constitute the fairly recent art of the confectioner.

Mixed with milk, it produces the various creams and blancmanges whose delicate and ethereal flavour makes such a welcome change after the substantial taste of meat.

Mixed with coffee, it brings out the full aroma of that beverage.

Mixed with coffee and milk, it makes a light, agreeable and easily procurable form of nourishment, most suitable for those persons who have to begin work immediately after breakfast. Coffee and milk is also a source of supreme pleasure to the ladies; but the perceptive eye of science has observed that excessive indulgence in it may prove harmful to that which they hold most dear.

Mixed with fruit and flowers, it produces jam, marmalade, preserves, jellies, pastes, and candies, enabling us to enjoy the fragrance of those fruits and flowers long after the period fixed by Nature for their duration. In this connexion, sugar might also be used to advantage in the art of embalming, which is still in a rudimentary stage in our civilization.

Finally, sugar mixed with alcohol produces spirituous liqueurs, which as everyone knows were invented to put new ardour into the aged Louis XIV, and which, by their forceful effect on the palate and their fragrant fumes, form the *nec plus ultra* of gastronomic delight.

These are not all the uses of sugar. It may be said to be the universal condiment, which never spoils anything. There are people who use it with meat, sometimes with vegetables, and often with fresh fruit. It is essential to the mixed drinks which are so fashionable today, such as punch, negus, syllabub, and others of exotic origin; and its applications are of infinite variety, since they can be modified to suit the tastes of peoples and individuals.

Such is this substance, the very name of which was almost unknown to the Frenchmen of the time of Louis XIII, yet which has become a prime necessity to those of the nineteenth century; for there is scarcely a woman, especially a woman of means, who does not spend more on sugar than on bread.

Monsieur Delacroix, that charming and prolific author, was once heard at Versailles to complain of the price of sugar, which at that time was over five francs a pound. 'Ah,' he said in melting tones, 'if ever sugar comes down to thirty sous again, then as long as I live I shall never drink water without sugar in it.'

His hopes were fulfilled; he is still alive, and I trust that he has kept his word.

ORIGIN OF COFFEE

The first coffee-tree was found in Arabia, and in spite of the various transplantations which that shrub has since undergone, Arabia still remains the source of the best coffee.

According to an old tradition coffee was discovered by a goat-herd, who noticed a strange restlessness and hilarity in his flock whenever they had browsed on coffee-berries.

Even if that legend is true, however, only half the honour of the discovery would belong to the observant goat-herd; the other half must be allowed to the first man who thought of applying heat to the beans. For the decoction of crude coffee is a mediocre beverage; but carbonization develops the aroma and oil which are the characteristic of coffee as we drink it today; and these qualities would never have been known without the application of heat.

The Turks, who are our masters in this matter, never use a mill to grind their coffee beans; they pound them in mortars with wooden pestles; and when those instruments have been used for a long time, they become valuable and are sold at a high price.

I felt it incumbent on me, for several reasons, to find out whether there was any difference between the results obtained by the two methods, and if so, which was to be preferred. Accordingly I carefully roasted a pound of pure Mocha, and divided it into two equal parts, one of which was then ground in a mill, and the other pounded after the Turkish fashion.

I made coffee with each of the two powders; I took an

equal quantity of each; and on each I poured an equal quantity of boiling water, conducting the whole operation with absolute impartiality.

I tasted the two coffees, and also submitted them to the most eminent connoisseurs. The unanimous verdict was that the coffee made with the pounded powder was clearly superior to that made from the ground beans.

Anyone is at liberty to repeat the experiment. Meanwhile I can cite a curious example of the different effects obtained from different methods of manipulation.

'Monsieur,' Napoleon said one day to Senator Laplace, 'why is it that a glass of water in which I dissolve a lump of sugar seems so much better than one in which I place a like quantity of powdered sugar?'

'Sire,' replied the scientist, 'there are three substances whose elements are identical, namely, sugar, gum and starch; they only differ in certain conditions, the secret of which Nature keeps to herself; and I think it possible that under the action of the pestle, a few portions of the powdered sugar assume the character of gum or starch, and cause the difference which occurs in that case.'

This anecdote received some publicity at the time, and subsequent investigations have confirmed the accuracy of the Senator's observation.

Different Ways of Making Coffee

A few years ago all minds were simultaneously turned to the problem of finding the best way of making coffee, a phenomenon which, though no one suspected it, was probably due to the fact that the head of the Government was extremely partial to that beverage.

It was suggested that it should be made without roasting it, without reducing it to powder, by infusing it cold, by boiling it for three quarters of an hour, by placing it in a sealed boiler, and so on.

In my time I have tried every one of these methods and all the others which have been put forward down to the present day, and my considered opinion is that the best of all is the method called *à la Dubelloy*, which consists in placing the coffee in a porcelain or silver receptacle pierced with very small holes, and pouring boiling water over it. This first decoction is brought to boiling-point again, and again passed through the strainer, after which the coffee will be as clear and as good as possible.

In one of my experiments I tried to make coffee in a high-pressure boiler; but the result was a mixture of extractive matter and bitterness, fit for nothing but a Cossack's gullet.

Effects of Coffee

Learned doctors have expressed a variety of opinions concerning the sanitary properties of coffee, and have not always seen eye to eye; we will steer clear of the fray, and turn our attention only to the most important of them all, namely its influence on the organs of thought.

It is beyond doubt that coffee causes considerable excitement in the brain; and anyone drinking it for the first time is certain to be robbed of some of his sleep.

Sometimes this effect is softened or modified by habit; but there are many individuals who always remain subject to this excitement, and are consequently obliged to give up drinking coffee altogether.

I have said that the effect may be modified by habit, but this does not prevent it from occurring in another form; for I have observed that those persons who are not prevented by coffee from sleeping at night need it to keep awake by day, and never fail to fall asleep during the evening when they have not taken any coffee after dinner.

There are many others, moreover, who are sleepy all day long when they have not drunk their cup of coffee in the morning. Voltaire and Buffon were great coffee-drinkers and perhaps derived from that practice, one, the admirable clarity which is in all his works, and the other, the fervent harmony of his style. It is evident that several passages in the *Essays on Man*, about the dog, the tiger, the lion, and the horse, were written in a state of extreme cerebral exaltation.

The insomnia caused by coffee is not distressing; one's perceptions are sharper and one has no wish to sleep; that is all. There is none of the agitation and unhappiness which accompany insomnia brought on by any other cause; nevertheless, this untimely excitement may prove very dangerous in the long run.

In the old days, only people of mature years drank coffee; now everyone drinks it, and it may be the sting of its mental lash which drives such a huge crowd to take the roads leading to Olympus and the Temple of Memory. The cobbler author of the tragedy of *The Queen of Palmyra*, which all Paris heard read a few years ago, was greatly addicted to coffee; he therefore rose higher than the joiner of Nevers, who was nothing but a drunkard.

Coffee is a far more powerful liquor than is commonly

believed. A man of sound constitution can drink two bottles of wine a day, and live to a great age; the same man could not stand a like quantity of coffee for the same period; he would go out of his mind or die of consumption.

I once saw a man in London, in Leicester Square, who had been crippled by immoderate indulgence in coffee; he was no longer in any pain, having grown accustomed to his condition, and had cut himself down to five or six cups a day.

It is the duty of all papas and mammas to forbid their children to drink coffee, unless they wish to have little dried-up machines, stunted and old at the age of twenty. This warning is particularly directed to Parisians, whose children are not always as strong and healthy as if they had been born in other parts of the country, such as the Department of the Ain.

I myself am one of those who have been forced to give up coffee, and I will end this chapter by relating how one day I fell completely beneath its spell.

The Duc de Massa, at that time Minister of Justice, had asked me to undertake a piece of work which called for the closest application; he had given me very short notice, for he wanted it the following day.

I therefore resigned myself to a night's work; and in order to guard against the risk of falling asleep, I fortified my dinner with two large cups of strong aromatic coffee.

I came home at seven o'clock, having been told to expect the relevant papers about that time; but instead I found a letter informing me that, owing to some official formality, I would not receive them until the following morning.

Thus disappointed, in the full meaning of the term, I returned to the house at which I had dined, and played a game of piquet without experiencing any of the distractions to which I am usually subject.

For this I praised the coffee; but while enjoying the advantage it had given me, I was not without anxiety as to how I was to pass the night. However, I went to bed at the usual time, thinking that even if my slumbers were not as sound as they might be, I would at least sleep four or five hours, which would carry me gently through to the following morning.

I was mistaken; after two hours in bed I was wider awake than ever, and in a state of lively mental activity. My brain was like a mill with all its wheels revolving, but nothing for them to grind.

I felt that I must make some use of this disposition or the need for sleep would never come; and so I spent the time by turning a short story, which I had recently read in an English book, into verse.

I soon finished it, and as I was still as wide awake as before, I started on a second, but in vain. My poetic ardour cooled at the end of a dozen lines, and I was forced to give up.

In the end I spent the whole night without sleeping a wink, or even dozing for a single moment; I got up, and spent the day in the same condition, which remained unchanged by either the food I ate or the work I had to do. Finally, when I lay down the next night at my accustomed hour, I calculated that I had not closed my eyes for forty hours.

ORIGIN OF CHOCOLATE

The first men who landed in America were driven there by the thirst for gold. At that time mines were almost the only known source of wealth; agriculture and trade were in their infancy, and political economy was as yet unborn. The Spaniards, then, found precious metals; but this discovery was in a sense a barren one, because metal falls in value in proportion to the quantity discovered, and we have many more active methods of increasing the wealth of the world.

But those lands, where the heat of the sun brings the fields to a state of extreme fertility, were found to be ideally suited to the cultivation of sugar and coffee; moreover, the potato, the indigo plant, vanilla, quinine, and cacao were discovered there, and these were real treasures.

If these discoveries took place despite the obstacles put in the way of curiosity by a jealous nation, it is reasonable to hope that they will be multiplied tenfold in the future, and that the researches of the scientists of old Europe in so many unexplored countries will enrich the three kingdoms, animal, vegetable, and mineral, with a host of new substances, some of which, like vanilla, will provide us with new sensations, and others, like cacao, with new alimentary resources.

What we call *chocolate* is made by cooking the kernel of the cacao bean with sugar and cinnamon; such is the classic definition of chocolate. Sugar is an integral part of it; for from the kernels alone only cacao-paste or cocoa is obtained, and not chocolate. When the delicious flavour of vanilla is added to the sugar, cinnamon, and cacao, the *nec plus ultra* is attained of the perfection to which this preparation can be brought.

It is to this small number of substances that taste and experience have reduced the numerous ingredients which had been successively tried as adjuncts to cocoa, such as pepper, pimento, aniseed, ginger, aciola, and others.

The cacao tree is indigenous in both the islands and mainland of South America; but it is now generally agreed that the trees which yield the best fruit are those growing on the banks of the Maracaibo, in the valleys of Caracas, and the rich province of Sokomusco. There the kernel of the bean is larger, and the flavour sweeter and more concentrated. Since these regions became more accessible, it has been possible to make daily comparisons, and trained palates are now unerring in their choice.

The Spanish ladies of the New World love chocolate to the point of madness; not content with drinking it several times a day, they sometimes order it to be brought to them in church. This sensual indulgence often attracted the censure of the bishops, but they eventually closed their eyes to it, and the Reverend Father Escobar, whose metaphysics were as subtle as his morality was accommodating, formally declared that liquid chocolate was not a breach of fasting, thus stretching for the benefit of his fair penitents the ancient proverb: *Liquidum non frangit jejunum.**

---

* 'Liquid does not break a fast.' [Ed.]

Chocolate was introduced into Spain about the beginning of the seventeenth century, and its use rapidly became popular, owing to the predilection which women and monks, especially the latter, showed for this aromatic drink. Life in Spain has not changed in this respect and to this day chocolate is the principal refreshment on social occasions throughout the Peninsula.

Chocolate crossed the mountains with Anne of Austria, the daughter of Philip II and wife of Louis XIII. The Spanish monks also made it known by making presents of it to their French brethren, and successive Spanish ambassadors helped to bring it into fashion too. At the beginning of the Regency it was in more general use than coffee, because in those days it was taken as an agreeable form of nourishment, while coffee was still regarded as a rare and costly drink.

It is well known that Linnaeus called cacao *cacao theobroma*, the drink of the gods. Attempts have been made to find a reason for this emphatic qualification; some attribute it to his passionate predilection for chocolate; others to his desire to please his confessor; still others a wish to flatter the queen who had first introduced the custom. (*Incertum*)

Properties of Chocolate

The nature and properties of chocolate, and its place in the category of foods hot, cold, or cool, have been the occasion of solemn dissertations; but it must be admitted that these learned studies have contributed very little to the manifestation of truth.

However, time and experience, those two great

teachers, have conclusively proved that chocolate, when carefully prepared, is a wholesome and agreeable form of food; that it is nourishing and easily digestible; that unlike coffee, of which indeed it is the antidote, it holds no terrors for the fair sex; that it is very suitable for persons faced with great mental exertion, preachers, lawyers, and above all travellers; and finally that it agrees with the feeblest stomachs, has proved beneficial in cases of chronic illness, and remains the last resource in diseases of the pylorus.

Chocolate owes these various properties to the fact that as it is just an *eleosaccharum*, few substances contain such a high proportion of alimentary particles, so that it is almost entirely animalizable.

During the war* cacao was difficult to obtain and very expensive; efforts were made to find a substitute, but all in vain; and one of the blessings of peace has been the disappearance of the various brews which we had to drink out of politeness, but which were no more chocolate than an infusion of chicory is Mocha coffee.

There are some people who complain of being unable to digest chocolate, and others who, on the contrary, declare that it contains too little nourishment, and passes too quickly through the system.

It is extremely likely that the former have only themselves to blame, and that the chocolate they drink is of poor quality or badly prepared; for good chocolate well made should agree with any stomach in which there remains the smallest vestige of digestive power.

* The Napoleonic Wars. [Ed.]

As for the others, there is a simple remedy; let them reinforce their breakfast with a small meat pasty, a cutlet, or a broiled kidney, wash it all down with a good bowl of *Sokomusco*, and thank God for providing them with an active stomach.

This gives me an opportunity to insert an observation which can be relied on as absolutely exact.

When you have breakfasted well and copiously, if you swallow a generous cup of good chocolate at the end of the meal, you will have digested everything perfectly three hours later, and you will be able to dine in comfort . . . Out of zeal for science, and by dint of eloquence, I have persuaded a good many ladies to try this experiment, although they protested that it would kill them; in every case they were delighted with the result, and none of them failed to pay due tribute to the Professor.

Persons who drink chocolate regularly are conspicuous for unfailing health and immunity from the host of minor ailments which mar the enjoyment of life; they are also less inclined to lose weight; these are two advantages which anyone may verify in his own circle of acquaintances and among people whose diet can be ascertained.

This is the right place to speak of the properties of chocolate flavoured with amber; properties which I have verified in a great many experiments, the result of which I am proud to lay before my readers.

So let any man who has drunk too deeply of the cup of pleasure, or given to work a notable portion of the time which should belong to sleep; who finds his wit temporarily losing its edge, the atmosphere humid, time dragging, and the air hard to breathe, or who is tortured by a fixed idea which robs him of all freedom of thought; let such a man, we say, administer to himself a good pint of ambered chocolate, allowing between sixty and seventy-two grains of amber to a pound, and he will see wonders.

In my own peculiar way of specifying things, I call ambered chocolate 'the chocolate of the afflicted', because in each of the various conditions listed above there is a feeling hard to define but *common to them all*, which resembles affliction.

Difficulty of Making Good Chocolate

Very good chocolate is made in Spain; but we have stopped importing it from that country, because the Spanish makers are not all equally skilful, and the customer is forced to drink what he receives, whether it is good or bad.

Italian chocolate is not much to the French taste; generally speaking, the cacao is over-roasted, which makes the chocolate bitter and insufficiently nutritious, because part of the kernel has been burnt up.

Now that drinking chocolate has become universally popular in France, everyone has tried his hand at making it, but few have attained perfection, because the process is very far from being easy.

First of all, you must be able to tell good cacao from bad, and be determined to use only the best; for not even the finest quality cacao is entirely free from blemish, and misguided self-interest often overlooks damaged kernels, which should be thrown out to obtain the best results. The roasting of cacao is another delicate operation, and demands a certain tact not far removed from inspiration. There are some workers who are born with this skill and who never make mistakes.

A special talent is also needed for the proper regulation of the quantity of sugar which must go into the composition; no invariable rule can be laid down, for the amount must be varied according to the flavour of the kernels, and the degree of heat to which the cacao has been brought.

The grinding and mixing demands no less care, for it is on their absolute perfection that the digestibility of the chocolate partly depends.

Other considerations must govern the choice and quantity of the flavouring, which cannot be the same for chocolate intended to be taken as food, and for chocolate intended to be eaten as a sweet. It will also depend on whether or not vanilla is to be added to the mixture; so that, in order to make exquisite chocolate, a number of very subtle equations must be solved, which we profit by without even being aware of their existence.

For some time now, machines have been used for making chocolate; we do not believe that this method adds anything to its perfection, but it achieves a great saving of labour, and those who have adopted this method should be able to sell their chocolate cheaper. The contrary, however, seems to be the case; and this shows all too clearly that the real spirit of commerce is not yet naturalized in France, for in all fairness the advantage obtained by the use of machines should be equally profitable to the merchant and the consumer.

Being ourselves very fond of chocolate, we have run the gamut of nearly all the dealers, and we have now settled upon Monsieur Debauve, of No. 26 Rue des Saints-Pères; he is a purveyor of chocolate to the King, and we rejoice to see that the sun's rays have lighted on the worthiest of all. There is nothing surprising about that; Monsieur Debauve is a distinguished pharmacist, and brings to his chocolate-making all the learning he had acquired for use in a wider sphere.

Those who have never used their hands can have no idea of the difficulties which must be overcome before perfection can be attained in any material, nor of how much care, skill, and experience are needed to produce chocolate which is sweet but not insipid, strong but not bitter, aromatic but not sickly, and thick but free from sediment.

Such are the qualities of Monsieur Debauve's chocolate; it owes its supremacy to a sound choice of materials, a firm determination to allow nothing inferior to leave his factory, and the keen eye of the proprietor which watches over every detail of the work.

Following the guidance of sound doctrine, Monsieur Debauve has also endeavoured to supply his numerous customers with palatable antidotes against certain minor ailments.

Thus, to persons lacking in flesh he offers a body-building chocolate, flavoured with salep; to those whose nerves are weak, anti-spasmodic chocolate, flavoured with orange-blossom; to irritable persons, almond-milk chocolate; and to this list he will doubtless add 'chocolate for the afflicted' prepared with amber *secundum artem*.

But his supreme merit consists in his offering, at a modest price, an excellent everyday chocolate, which is enough in itself for our morning breakfast, delights us at dinner with our creams, and enchants us yet again at the end of the evening with our ices, and sweets, and other drawing-room dainties, not to mention the amusing distraction of crackers with or without mottoes.

Our only acquaintance with Monsieur Debauve is through his wares; we have never set eyes on him; but we know that he is helping considerably to free France from the tribute she used to pay to Spain, by providing Paris and the provinces with a chocolate whose reputation is constantly increasing. We also know that every day he receives new orders from abroad; and it is on these grounds, and as a founder member of the Society for the Encouragement of National Industry, that we here accord him a form of honourable mention of which the reader will discover that we are anything but prodigal.

Official Method of Preparing Chocolate

The Americans prepare their cacao in the form of an unsweetened paste without sugar; when they wish to make chocolate they send for boiling water; each person scrapes into his cup as much cacao as he requires, pours the hot water over it, and adds sugar and flavouring to suit his taste.

This method is contrary to both our habits and our tastes; we prefer the chocolate to reach us ready prepared. Transcendental chemistry informs us that in this condition it must neither be scraped with a knife nor crushed with a pestle, because the collision which takes place in these two cases starches certain portions of the sugar and makes the drink insipid.

So, to make chocolate, that is to say, to prepare it for immediate consumption, take about one and a half ounces for each cup of water, and let it dissolve slowly while the water comes to the boil, stirring it with a wooden spatula; let it boil for a quarter of an hour, to give the solution consistency, and serve piping hot.

Over fifty years ago Madame d'Arestrel, Superior of the Convent of the Visitation at Belley, said to me: 'Monsieur, when you wish to drink good chocolate, have it made the day before in a porcelain coffee-pot, and left overnight: The night's rest concentrates it, and God cannot frown on this little refinement, for He is himself all excellence.'

The Theory of Frying

It was a fine day in the month of May; the sun was shedding its gentlest rays on the smoke-begrimed roofs of the city of pleasures, and for once there was neither dust nor mud in the streets.

The great mail-coaches had long since ceased to rumble over the cobblestones; the heavy carts were still at rest, and the only vehicles at large were those open carriages from which fair ladies, both indigenous and exotic, sheltered beneath the most elegant of hats, are accustomed to glance disdainfully at the ugly and coquettishly at the handsome.

In short, it was three o'clock in the afternoon when the Professor settled down in his chair of meditation.

His right leg rested vertically on the floor; his left was stretched out diagonally; his back was suitably supported, and his hands lay on the lion's-head extremities of the arms of that venerable chair.

His lofty brow revealed a love of serious study, his mouth a taste for pleasant distractions. His demeanour was calm and his bearing such that no one seeing him could have failed to say: 'This old man must surely be a sage.'

Thus seated, the Professor summoned his chief cook; and soon the servant appeared, ready to receive advice, instruction, or commands.

Address

'Maître la Planche,' said the Professor in those grave tones which go straight to the heart, 'all who sit at my table proclaim you a soup-maker of the highest order, and that is well, for soup is the first consolation of a hungry stomach; but I note with sorrow that in the art of frying you have still a lot to learn.

'Yesterday I heard you groaning over that triumphal sole which you served up all pale, flabby, and discoloured. My friend R—* looked at you disapprovingly; Monsieur H. R. pointed his gnomonic nose to the west, and President Sibuet wept over the dish as if it were a national disaster.

'This misfortune befell you because you disregarded theory, failing to appreciate its importance. You are a little stubborn, and I find it hard to convince you that the phenomena which occur in your laboratory are simply the fulfilment of the eternal laws of nature, and that certain things which you do carelessly, and only because you have seen others do them, none the less possess the loftiest scientific origins.

'Listen carefully then, and learn, so that you may never again have cause to blush over your handiwork.'

---

* Monsieur R—, born in Seysell, a district of Belley, about 1757. An elector of the *grand collège*, he may be cited as a striking example of the happy outcome of prudent behaviour combined with the most inflexible probity.

Chemistry

'Not all the liquids which you expose to the action of fire can be charged with an equal quantity of heat; Nature has made them unequally receptive; she alone knows the secret of this order of things, which we call *caloric capacity*.

'Thus, you could dip your finger into boiling spirits of wine with impunity; but you would withdraw it hastily from boiling brandy, and more quickly still from boiling water; while a brief immersion in boiling oil would cause you serious injury, for oil has at least three times the heating capacity of water.

'It is due to this state of affairs that hot liquids act differently on the sapid substances immersed in them. Those which are immersed in water grow soft, disintegrate, and finally turn to pulp: that is how broth or extracts are made. On the other hand, those which are immersed in oil shrink, take on varying degrees of colour, and in the end become entirely carbonized.

'In the first case, the water dissolves and absorbs the internal juices of the foodstuffs immersed in it; and in the second, those juices are preserved, because the oil cannot dissolve them; and if the substance dries up, it is because its humid parts have finally evaporated under the continued influence of heat.

'These two different processes also have different names: the process of boiling foodstuffs in oil or fat is called *frying*. I have said already, I believe, that for culinary purposes *oil* and *fat* are nearly synonymous, since fat is simply solidified oil, and oil is liquid fat.'

Applications of the Theory

'Fried foods are welcome at any banquet; they introduce an appetizing variety into the meal, and are pleasant to the eye; they retain their original flavour, and can be eaten with the fingers, a quality which is always appreciated by the ladies.

'Frying also provides cooks with countless means of disguising food which has already been served up the day before and stands them in good stead in unforeseen emergencies; for it takes no longer to fry a four-pound carp than to boil an egg.

'The whole merit of frying consists in the *surprise*; for such is the name given to the sudden action of the boiling liquid which carbonizes or scorches the surface of the substance in question, at the very moment of its immersion.

'By means of this *surprise* a sort of ceiling is formed over the object, which prevents the fat from penetrating it, and concentrates the juices inside, so that they undergo an internal cooking process which gives the dish all the flavour of which it is capable.

'The *surprise* will only occur when the liquid is so hot that its action is sudden and instantaneous; but it only reaches this point after fairly prolonged exposure to the heat of a blazing fire.

'The following method will show whether the fat has attained the required degree of heat: Cut a piece of bread into the form of a sippet and dip it in the frying-pan for five or six seconds; if it comes out crisp and brown, proceed immediately with the immersion; if not, you must stoke the fire and start the experiment all over again.

'Once the *surprise* has been effected, damp the fire down so that the cooking is not too rapid, and so that the juices you have imprisoned may undergo the influence of a sustained heat which draws them together and enhances their flavour.

'You have doubtless observed that the surface of well-fried foodstuffs will no longer dissolve salt or sugar, even though they need one or other of those substances. Therefore you will not fail to reduce the salt or sugar to a fine powder, so that it acquires an extreme adhesive quality, and, when sprinkled on fried food, seasons it by means of juxtaposition.

'I say nothing of the choice of oils and fats; you have already received sufficient enlightenment on that point from the various cookery books I have placed at your disposal.

'But do not forget that when you are given a few trout, each scarcely a quarter of a pound in weight, straight from some freshwater stream that murmurs far from the capital, do not forget, I say, to fry them in the finest olive oil at your command; this simple dish, salted, peppered, and adorned with slices of lemon, is worthy to be laid before an Eminence.*

'Give the same treatment to smelts, which are a special

---

* Monsieur Aulissin, a learned Neapolitan advocate and no mean performer on the cello, was dining with me one day when, eating something which pleased him greatly, he said: '*Questo è un vero boccone di cardinale!*' 'Why,' I replied, in the same tongue, 'don't you say, as we do, *a dish fit for a king?*' 'Monsieur,' he answered, 'we Italians consider that kings cannot be gourmands, because their meals are too short and solemn; but cardinals are a different matter!' And he gave that peculiar whooping chuckle of his: hou, hou, hou, hou, hou, hou!

joy to connoisseurs. The smelt is the warbler of the sea; fish and bird are alike in being small, delicate, and altogether superior.

'These two prescriptions are founded on the nature of things. Experience has taught us that olive oil should only be used in operations which can be performed within a short space of time, or which require no great heat, because prolonged boiling invests it with an empyreumatic and unpleasant taste, due to the presence of certain particles of parenchyma, which are very difficult to get rid of, and which become carbonized.

'You have ventured into my infernal regions, and you have known the glory of being the first man to offer to an astounded world a huge fried turbot; that day was a day of jubilation among the elect.

'Go then: continue to take care over all you do, and never forget that from the moment guests set foot in my dining-room, it is *we* who are responsible for their well-being.'

On Drinks*

INTRODUCTION

The word drink is used of any liquid which can be used to accompany our food.

Water seems to be the most natural drink. It is found wherever there are animals, takes the place of milk among adults, and is no less necessary to us than air.

Water

Water is the only drink which really quenches thirst, and that is the reason why it can only be drunk in comparatively small quantities. Most of the other liquors which man imbibes are only palliatives, and if he had confined himself to water, it would never have been said of him that one of his privileges was to drink without being thirsty.

The Prompt Effect of Drinks

Drinks are absorbed into the animal economy with extreme ease; their effect is prompt, and the relief which they give almost instantaneous. Lay a substantial meal before a tired man, and he will eat with difficulty and be

---

* This chapter is purely philosophical; a detailed account of the various known drinks could not be included in my work as planned; there would have been no end to it.

little the better for it at first. Give him a glass of wine or brandy, and immediately he feels better: you see him come to life again before you.

A curious occurrence, of which my nephew, Colonel Guigard, told me, lends support to this theory. My nephew is no storyteller by nature, but the truth of his tale is beyond question.

He was at the head of a detachment returning from the siege of Jaffa, and they had reached a point only a few hundred paces from the place where they were due to make a halt and find some water when they noticed some dead bodies on the road; they were the corpses of some soldiers belonging to a detachment a day's march ahead of my nephew's, who had died of the heat.

Among the victims of that burning climate was a carabineer who was known to several of my nephew's men. He had presumably been dead for over twenty-four hours, and the sun, beating down on him all day, had turned his face as black as a crow.

Some of his comrades came over to the body, either to look at him one last time, or to collect their inheritance, if there was anything to inherit; and they were aston-ished to find his limbs still flexible; and even a little warmth in the neighbourhood of the heart.

'Give him a drop of *sacré-chien*,' said the wag of the detachment; 'I'll bet that unless he's gone a long way into the next world, he'll come back for a taste of that.'

Sure enough, at the first spoonful of spirits the dead man opened his eyes; everyone cried out in amazement; and after his temples had been rubbed with the spirits and he had been given a little more to drink, he was able, with some assistance, to keep his seat on a donkey.

They led him like this to the well; during the night he was looked after carefully, and given a few dates to eat, with some other light food; and the following day, again mounted on the donkey, he reached Cairo with the rest.

STRONG DRINKS

A thing of enormous interest is that sort of instinct, as general as it is imperious, which leads us in search of strong drinks.

Wine, the most delightful of drinks, whether we owe it to Noah, who planted the vine, or to Bacchus, who pressed juice from the grape, dates from the childhood of the world; and beer, which is attributed to Osiris, goes back to a period beyond which nothing certain is known.

All men, even those it is customary to call savages, have been so tormented by this craving for strong drinks, that they have always managed to obtain them, however limited the extent of their knowledge.

They have turned the milk of their domestic animals sour, or extracted juice from various fruits and roots which they suspected of containing the elements of fermentation; and wherever human society has existed, we find that men were provided with strong liquors, which they used at their feasts, sacrifices, marriages, or funerals, in short on all occasions of merry-making or solemnity.

Wine was drunk and its praises sung for many centuries before men guessed at the possibility of extracting the spirituous part which makes its strength; but when the Arabs taught us the art of distillation, which they had invented for the purpose of extracting the scent of flowers, and above all that of the rose which occupies such an important place in their writings, then men began to believe that it was possible to discover in wine the cause of that special savour which has such a stimulating influence on the organ of taste; and so, step by step, alcohol, spirits of wine, and brandy were discovered.

Alcohol is the prince of liquids, and carries the palate to its highest pitch of exaltation; its various preparations have opened up a new source of pleasure;* it invests certain medicaments† with a power which they could not otherwise have attained; and it has even become a formidable weapon in our hands, for the nations of the New World have been subdued and destroyed almost as much by brandy as by firearms.

The method by which alcohol was discovered has led to other important results; for consisting as it does in the separation and exposure of the parts which make up a body, and distinguish that body from all others, it has served as a model to scholars pursuing analogous researches; and they have made known to us entirely new substances, such as strychnine, quinine, morphine, and others, both discovered and to be discovered in the future.

Be that as it may, this thirst for a kind of liquid which Nature has enveloped in veils, this strange desire that assails all the races of mankind, in every climate and

---

* Liqueurs. † Elixirs.

temperature, is most worthy to attract the attention of the philosophic observer.

I, among others, have pondered it, and I am tempted to place the craving for fermented liquors, which is unknown to animals, with anxiety regarding the future, which is likewise unknown to animals, and to regard both as distinctive attributes of the masterpiece of the last sublunary revolution.

On Gourmandism

I have consulted all the dictionaries about the word *Gourmandism*, and am far from satisfied with what I have found. There is endless confusion between *gourmandism*, properly so called, and *gluttony* or *voracity*; whence I conclude that lexicographers, excellent fellows though they may be in other respects, are not to be numbered among those charming scholars who eat a partridge wing with easy grace, and wash it down, little finger in the air, with a glass of Lafite or Glos Vougeot.

They have forgotten, utterly forgotten, social gourmandism, which combines the elegance of Athens, the luxury of Rome, and the delicacy of France, and which unites careful planning with skilled performance, gustatory zeal with wise discrimination; a precious quality, which might well be called a virtue, and is at least the source of our purest pleasures.

DEFINITIONS

Let us then define our terms and make ourselves clear.

Gourmandism is an impassioned, reasoned, and habitual preference for everything which gratifies the organ of taste.

Gourmandism is the enemy of excess; indigestion

and drunkenness are offences which render the offender liable to be struck off the rolls.

Gourmandism includes *friandise*, which is simply the same preference applied to light, delicate, and insubstantial food, such as preserves and pastry. It is a modification introduced in favour of the ladies and those gentlemen who resemble them.

From whatever point of view gourmandism is considered, it deserves nothing but praise and encouragement.

From the physical point of view, it is the result and proof of the sound and perfect condition of the organs of nourishment.

From the moral point of view, it shows implicit obedience to the commands of the Creator, who, when He ordered us to eat in order to live, gave us the inducement of appetite, the encouragement of savour, and the reward of pleasure.

ADVANTAGES OF GOURMANDISM

From the point of view of political economy, gourmandism is the common bond which unites the nations of the world, through the reciprocal exchange of objects serving for daily consumption.

It is gourmandism which sends wines, spirits, sugar, spices, pickles, salted foods, and provisions of every kind, down to eggs and melons, across the earth from pole to pole.

It is gourmandism which determines the relative price of things mediocre, good, and excellent, whether their qualities are the effect of art or the gift of nature.

It is gourmandism which sustains the hopes and the spirit of rivalry of the host of fishermen, huntsmen, farmers, and others who every day fill the richest larders with the result of their labours and discoveries.

And lastly, it is gourmandism which forms the livelihood of the industrious throng of cooks, confectioners, bakers, and others of all descriptions concerned with the preparation of food, who in their turn employ other works of every kind for their needs, thus giving rise at all times to a circulation of funds incalculable in respect to mobility and magnitude by even the most expert brains.

Let it be remembered too that the industry which has gourmandism as its object enjoys the special advantage that it depends on the one hand on the greatest fortunes and on the other on the recurring needs of everyday life.

In the present state of society it is difficult to imagine a race which could live on bread and vegetables alone. Such a race, if it existed, would infallibly be subjugated by any carnivorous army, like the Hindus, who have successively fallen prey to all their assailants; or else it would be converted by the skill in cookery of its neighbours, like the Boeotians of old, who became gourmands after the battle of Leuctra.

MORE ADVANTAGES

Gourmandism also has considerable fiscal importance; toll dues, customs duties, and indirect taxes thrive on it. Everything we consume pays tribute, and gourmands are the chief mainstay of every nation's wealth.

What shall we say of the swarm of cooks who for centuries past have left France to exploit the gourmandism of other lands? Most of them succeed in their endeavours, and obeying an instinct which never dies in a Frenchman's heart, bring back to their native soil the fruits of their economy. This access of wealth is more important than might be imagined, and these men, like the others, will have their genealogical tree.

If nations were grateful, none would have better reason than France to raise altars and a temple to Gourmandism.

THE POWER OF GOURMANDISM

In 1815, under the November Treaty,* France was required to pay seven hundred and fifty millions† to the Allies in three years.

A further condition required her to meet the individual claims of the inhabitants of the various Allied countries, which, with the interest fixed by the sovereigns of those powers, amounted to over three hundred millions.‡

Finally, to this must be added the requisitions of all kinds made by the enemy generals, which they sent off in cartloads to the frontiers, and which later had to be

---

* This was the Second Treaty of Paris (the first had been signed in 1814), the final settlement of the Napoleonic Wars. [Translator.]
† It is difficult to estimate equivalent values, but this sum represents approximately £180 m. in 1970. [Translator.]
‡ Approximately £72 m. in 1970. [Translator.]

paid for out of the public purse; in all, over fifteen hundred millions.*

There was every reason to fear that such considerable payments, which were made day after day *in cash*, might put an intolerable strain on the exchequer, and cause a depreciation of all fictitious values, followed by all the misfortunes which overwhelm a penniless country deprived of the means of obtaining money.

'Alas,' said men of property, as they watched the fatal tumbril going to be loaded up in the Rue Vivienne, 'alas, there goes our money on its way out of the country; next year, we shall go down on our knees before a crown piece; we shall be ruined and reduced to beggary, all enterprises will fail; borrowing will be impossible; and we shall be faced with decline, stagnation, and civil death.'

Events gave the lie to these fears, and to the amazement of all students of finance, the payments were made with ease, credit improved, loans were oversubscribed, and during the whole period of this superpurgation the rate of exchange, that infallible index of the circulation of money, remained in our favour; in other words, there was mathematical proof that more money was coming into France than going out of it.

What was the power which came to our aid? What divinity performed this miracle?

Gourmandism.

When the Britons, the Germans, the Teutons, the Cimmerians, and the Scythians poured into France, they

---

* Approximately £360 m. in 1970. [Translator.]

brought with them a rare voracity and stomachs of uncommon capacity.

· They were not content for long with the official cheer forthcoming from forced hospitality; they aspired to more delicate pleasures; and before long the queen of cities had become a vast refectory. These intruders ate in restaurants, in hotels, in taverns, at street-stalls, and even in the streets.

They stuffed themselves with meat, fish, game, truffles, pastry, and above all with our fruit.

Their thirst was as insatiable as their appetite; and they always asked for the most expensive wines, in the hope of discovering unheard-of joys, which they were subsequently astonished not to experience.

Superficial observers did not know what to think of this endless feasting for no reason; but the true Frenchman laughed and rubbed his hands, saying: 'They are under a spell, and by tonight they will have paid us back more crowns than the Treasury handed over to them this morning.'

It was a golden time for all who ministered to the pleasures of taste. Véry finished making his fortune; Achard laid the foundations of his; Beauvilliers amassed his third, and Madame Sulot, whose shop in the Palais-Royal was only a few feet square, sold up to twelve thousand tarts a day.*

---

* When the army of invasion passed through Champagne, it took six hundred thousand bottles of wine from Monsieur Moët's cellars at Épernay, a town famed for the beauty of its cellars. He soon found consolation for this enormous loss; for the looters acquired a taste for his wines, and the orders which he receives from the North have more than doubled since that time.

The influence of that period has continued to this day; foreigners come pouring in from every part of Europe to resume in peacetime the pleasant habits which they acquired during the war; they must come to Paris; and when they are there they must indulge their tastes, no matter what the cost. And if our public bonds are in favour, it is due not so much to the high rate of interest they carry, as to the instinctive confidence everyone inevitably feels in a people in whose midst gourmands are happy.*

PORTRAIT OF A PRETTY GOURMAND

Gourmandism is by no means unbecoming in women; it suits the delicacy of their organs, and compensates in some degree for the pleasures they must forgo, and the ills to which Nature seems to have condemned them.

There is no more charming sight than a pretty gourmand in action: her napkin is daintily tucked in; one hand rests on the table; the other conveys to her mouth elegantly cut morsels, or a wing of partridge for her teeth to bite; her eyes are bright, her lips glistening, and all her movements full of grace; and she does not lack that touch of coquetry which women show in everything they do. With such advantages she is irresistible, and even Cato the Censor could not look at her unmoved.

---

* The calculations on which this chapter is based were furnished by Monsieur M.B., an aspirant to gastronomical distinction, who is not without qualifications, being a financier and a music-lover.

Anecdote

But here a bitter memory comes to mind.

One day, being placed next to pretty Madame M—d at table, I was inwardly rejoicing at my good fortune, when she suddenly turned to me and said: 'Your health!' I promptly began a neat reply, but I never finished, for the coquette turned towards her other neighbour, and asked him to drink with her. They touched glasses; and that left a wound in my heart which many years have failed to heal.

Women are Gourmands

There is something instinctive in the penchant for gourmandism which prevails among the fair sex, for gourmandism is favourable to beauty.

A series of exact and rigorous observations has shown that a succulent, delicate, and well-chosen diet delays the outward signs of old age for a long time.

It lends new brilliance to the eyes, new bloom to the skin, and new strength to the muscles; and as it is certain, physiologically, that slackening of the muscles is the cause of wrinkles, those dread enemies of beauty, it is no less true to say that, all things being equal, those who know how to eat look ten years younger than those to whom that science is a mystery.

Painters and sculptors are well aware of this truth, for they never depict a person who fasts out of choice or duty, such as a miser or an anchorite, without giving him the pallor of sickness, the thinness of poverty, and the wrinkles of decrepitude.

EFFECTS OF GOURMANDISM
ON SOCIABILITY

Gourmandism is one of the principal bonds of society; for it is gourmandism that gradually draws out that convivial spirit which every day brings all sorts together, moulds them into a single whole, sets them talking, and rounds off the sharp corners of conventional inequality.

It is gourmandism too which inspires the efforts every good host must make to entertain his guests, and the gratitude of his guests when they see what pains have been taken on their behalf; and this is the place to cry eternal shame on those stupid eaters who swallow the choicest dainties with culpable indifference, or breathe in with sacrilegious insouciance the fragrance of a limpid nectar.

General Law

Any display of ingenious hospitality calls for an explicit eulogy; and wherever the desire to please is evident, a word of praise is customary.

INFLUENCE OF GOURMANDISM
ON CONJUGAL HAPPINESS

Finally, gourmandism, when it is shared, has the most marked influence on the happiness which may be found in the married state.

Two married gourmands have a pleasant opportunity to meet at least once a day; for even those who sleep apart (and there are many such) eat at the same table; they have a subject of conversation which never grows stale, for they talk not only about what they are eating, but also of what they have eaten, what they are about to eat, what they have observed at other houses, fashionable dishes, new culinary inventions, etc., etc.; and such chit-chat is full of charm.

No doubt music too has strong attractions for those who love it; but it must be played, and that requires an effort. Besides, a cold, a lost music-book, an instrument out of tune, or even a headache, and there is no music.

But a common need calls man and wife to table, and a common inclination keeps them there; they naturally show each other those little courtesies which reveal a desire to please; and the manner in which meals are conducted is an important ingredient in the happiness of life.

This last piece of wisdom, which is new to France, did not escape the English moralist, Richardson; he enlarges on it in his novel *Pamela*, where he depicts the different ways in which two married couples spend their day.

The two husbands are brothers; the elder is a peer in full possession of the family estate; the younger is Pamela's husband, disinherited on account of this marriage, and living on the proceeds of his half-pay in straitened circumstances not far removed from poverty.

The peer and his lady enter their dining-room from opposite directions, and greet each other coldly, although it is their first meeting of the day. They sit down at a lavishly spread table, surrounded by lackeys gleaming with gold; they help themselves in silence and eat without zest. However, when the servants have withdrawn, a kind of conversation begins between them; but sharp words are exchanged, a quarrel ensues, and the pair rise from table in a fury, to seek their separate rooms, where each thinks of the sweetness of the widowed state.

The younger brother, on the other hand, on reaching his humble lodging, is welcomed with tender effusion and the sweetest of caresses. He sits down at a frugal board; but the excellence of his meal is assured, for Pamela herself has cooked it. They eat with delight, chatting about their affairs, their projects, and their love. A half-bottle of Madeira serves to prolong both meal and conversation; then the same bed receives them both, and after the transports of mutual love, sweet slumber brings them forgetfulness of the present and dreams of better days to come.

All honour to gourmandism, such as we describe it to our readers, as long as it does not make a man lazy or extravagant! For just as the vices of Sardanapalus have not turned men against women, so the excesses of Vitellius should make no man turn his back on a well-chosen, ordered feast.

When gourmandism becomes gluttony, greed, and debauchery, it loses both its name and its advantages; it then falls outside our province and enters that of the moralist, who will treat it with his counsel, or of the doctor, who will cure it with his drugs.

La gourmandise as the Professor has described it in this chapter, has no name except in French; it cannot be rendered by the Latin *gula*, nor the English *gluttony*, nor the German *Lüsternheit*; and we therefore advise anyone who might be tempted to translate this instructive work to retain the word unchanged; that is what all other nations have done with *la coquetterie* and the words derived from it.

Note by a Patriotic Gourmand

I note with pride that coquetry and gourmandism, those two great modifications which extreme sociability have made to our most pressing needs, are both of French origin.

On the Pleasures of the Table

INTRODUCTION

It is certain that more pain is felt by man than by all the other sentient creatures which inhabit our globe.

Nature condemned him to suffering from the start through the nakedness of his skin, the shape of his feet, and the instinct of war and destruction which has every-where been found implanted in the human race.

The animals have not been stricken with this curse; and if it were not for such fighting as is caused by the instinct of reproduction, pain would be unknown to most species: whereas man, who can only experience pleasure intermittently, and through a small number of organs, may at all times, and through every part of his body, be subjected to appalling pain.

This decree of fate has been aggravated in its execu-tion by a host of ills caused by the habits of social life, so that the keenest and most satisfying pleasures imagin-able can never, either in intensity *or* duration, compensate for the atrocious pain caused by certain maladies, such as gout, toothache, acute rheumatism, and strangury, or the terrible tortures practised in certain lands.

It is this fear of pain which causes man, without even knowing it, to seek opposite extremes, and to cling desperately to the few pleasures which Nature has placed within his reach.

For the same reason he adds to their number, improves, perfects, and even worships them; for in pagan times, for many centuries, all the pleasures were secondary divinities, under the patronage of superior gods.

The severity of the new religions put an end to those personages; Bacchus, Diana, Cupid, and Comus are now nothing more than poetic memories; but the thing survives, and under the strictest of all faiths there is still merriment and feasting at marriages, baptisms, and even funerals.

ORIGIN OF THE PLEASURES OF THE TABLE

Meals, in the sense in which we understand the word, began with the second age of man; that is to say, as soon as he stopped living wholly on fruits. The dressing and distribution of meat necessarily brought each family together, as the father shared out the produce of his hunting among his children, and later, the grown-up children performed the same service for their aged parents.

These gatherings were at first confined to the closest relatives, but gradually came to include friends and neighbours.

Later, when the human race had spread far and wide, the weary traveller would sit down at these primitive meals, and tell what was happening in distant lands. Thus hospitality was born, with rites held sacred by every nation; for even the most savage tribe undertook to respect the life of him who had eaten its own bread and salt.

It was the meal which was responsible for the birth, or at least the elaboration of languages, not only because it was a continually recurring occasion for meetings, but also because the leisure which accompanies and succeeds the meal is naturally conducive to confidence and loquacity.

DIFFERENCE BETWEEN THE PLEASURES OF EATING AND THE PLEASURES OF THE TABLE

Such, in the nature of things, must have been the origin of the pleasures of the table, which must be carefully distinguished from their necessary antecedent, the pleasure of eating.

The pleasure of eating is the actual and direct sensation of a need being satisfied.

The pleasures of the table are considered sensations born of the various circumstances of fact, things, and persons accompanying the meal.

The pleasure of eating is common to ourselves and the animals, and depends on nothing but hunger and the means to satisfy it.

The pleasures of the table are peculiar to mankind, and depend on preliminary care over the preparation of the meal, the choice of the place, and the selection of the guests.

The pleasure of eating requires, if not hunger, at least appetite; the pleasures of the table, more often than not, are independent of the one and the other.

Both of these two conditions may be observed at any dinner.

At the beginning of the meal, and throughout the first course, each guest eats steadily, without speaking or paying attention to anything which may be said; whatever his position in society, he forgets everything to become nothing but a worker in the great factory of Nature. But when the need for food begins to be satisfied, then the intellect awakes, talk becomes general, a new order of things is initiated, and he who until then was a mere consumer of food, becomes a table companion of more or less charm, according to the qualities bestowed on him by the Master of all things.

EFFECTS

There are neither raptures, nor ecstasies, nor transports of bliss in the pleasures of the table; but they make up in duration what they lose in intensity, and are distinguished above all by the merit of inclining us towards all the other pleasures of life, or at least of consoling us for the loss of them.

In short, at the end of a good dinner, body and soul both enjoy a remarkable sense of well-being.

The physical effect is that the brain is refreshed, the face brightens up, the colouring is heightened, the eyes grow brighter, and a pleasant warmth pervades the limbs.

On Obesity

If I had been a qualified doctor, I would in the first place have written a monograph on obesity; then I would have established my empire in that sphere of the profession. I would thus have enjoyed the dual advantage of having the healthiest of people as my patients, and being daily besieged by the prettier half of the human race; for to acquire a perfect degree of plumpness, neither too much nor too little, is the life-study of every woman in the world.

What I have not done, another doctor will do: and if he is at once learned, discreet, and a handsome fellow, I guarantee that he will obtain miraculous successes.

*Exoriare aliquis nostris ex ossibus haeres!**

Meanwhile, I am going to lead the way; for a chapter on obesity is essential in a work which has man and his meals as its subject.

By *obesity* I mean that state of fatty congestion in which, without the individual being ill, his limbs gradually increase in volume and lose their original shape and harmony.

There is a type of obesity which is confined to the belly; I have never known an example to occur among

* 'From my dead bones may some heir arise!' [Ed.]

women; for they are generally made of softer stuff than men, and obesity, when it attacks them, spares no part of their person. I call this variety *gastrophory*, and those affected by it *gastrophors*. I myself am one of them; but although I am the bearer of a fairly prominent paunch, the lower part of my legs is still hard, and the sinews as loosely knit as those of an Arab horse.

For all that, I have always regarded my paunch as a redoubtable enemy; I have beaten it and reduced it to majestic proportions; but in order to beat it I had to fight it, and whatever merit this work contains, I owe to a struggle of thirty years duration.

I will begin with an extract from more than five hundred dialogues I have had at table with such of my neighbours as were either threatened or afflicted with obesity.

STOUT PARTY: Heavens! What delicious bread! Where do you get it?

MYSELF: From Monsieur Limet, in the Rue de Richelieu: he is baker to their Royal Highnesses the Duc d'Orléans and the Prince de Condé; I first went to him because his shop is nearby, and I am faithful to him because I have proclaimed him the best panificator in the world.

STOUT PARTY: I must remember that; I eat a great deal of bread, and for rolls such as these I would willingly do without all the rest.

ANOTHER STOUT PARTY: But what on earth are you doing, swallowing the liquid part of your soup, and leaving that delicious Carolina rice?

MYSELF: I am following a special diet.

STOUT PARTY: That's a poor diet, I can tell you! Rice is the joy of my life, together with flour, noodles, and things of that sort; there's nothing more nutritious, cheaper, or more easily digestible.

A VERY STOUT PARTY: Monsieur, be so good as to pass me those potatoes in front of you. At the rate they're disappearing I am afraid of being too late.

MYSELF: Monsieur, they are within your reach.

VERY STOUT PARTY: But aren't you going to help yourself? There are enough for both of us, and after us the deluge.

MYSELF: No thank you; to my mind the only value of potatoes is as a safeguard against starvation; apart from that, I know of nothing more utterly insipid.

VERY STOUT PARTY: What gastronomical heresy! There's nothing better than potatoes; I eat them in every conceivable form, and if any appear in the second course, whether *à la Lyonnaise* or *au soufflé* I here and now stake my claim to them.

STOUT LADY: You would be kindness itself if you would get them to pass me those Soissons haricot beans I see at the end of the table.

MYSELF [*after complying with her request while singing softly to a well-known tune*]:

> Happy the Soissons folk who grow
> That king of beans the haricot!

STOUT PARTY: You mustn't joke about them; they are a real source of wealth for the region. Paris pays large sums of money for them. And I beg leave also to praise those little marsh beans they call English beans;

when they are young and fresh, they are food for the gods.

MYSELF: Anathema on all beans, both haricot and English!

STOUT PARTY [*with a resolute air*]: That for your anathema! Anyone would think you were a whole council in yourself!

MYSELF [*to another stout lady*]: Allow me to congratulate you on your excellent health, Madame: it seems to me you have grown a little plumper since I last had the honour of seeing you.

STOUT LADY: That is doubtless due to my new diet.

MYSELF: How so?

STOUT LADY: For some time now I have taken to breakfasting off a very good rich soup, a bowlful big enough for two; and what soup! The spoon stands upright in it.

MYSELF [*to another*]: Madame, if your eyes don't deceive me, you will accept a little of this charlotte? Let me attack it for you.

STOUT LADY: Well, Monsieur, my eyes do deceive you; there are only two things here I really like, and they are both of the masculine gender: one is that rice-cake with the golden stripes, and the other that gigantic sponge-cake; for you must know that I adore all sweet cakes.

MYSELF [*to another*]: While they are talking politics over there, Madame, may I interrogate this frangipane tart on your behalf?

STOUT LADY: Please do: nothing agrees with me so well as pastry. We have a pastry-cook lodging with us at home, and I do believe my daughter and myself between us absorb the whole of the rent he pays us, and more besides.

MYSELF [*after looking at the young person*]: The diet obviously suits you to perfection: your daughter is a very beautiful person, with every advantage.

STOUT LADY: Yet, believe it or not, her girl friends sometimes tell her she is too fat.

MYSELF: Perhaps they say that out of envy . . .

STOUT LADY: Quite possibly. In any case, I am marrying her off soon, and the first baby will put everything to rights.

Through conversations such as these I elucidated a theory whose elements I had first elucidated outside mankind, namely that the chief cause of corpulence is a diet with starchy and farinaceous elements; and in this way I satisfied myself that the same diet is always followed by the same effect.

Sure enough, carnivorous animals never grow fat (consider wolves, jackals, birds of prey, crows, etc.).

Herbivorous animals do not grow fat easily, at least until age has reduced them to a state of inactivity; but they fatten very quickly as soon as they begin to be fed on potatoes, grain, or any kind of flour.

Obesity is never found either among the savages, or in those classes of society in which men work to eat, and eat only to live.

CAUSES OF OBESITY

From the observations noted above, the accuracy of which anyone can verify, it is easy to discover the principal causes of obesity.

The first is the natural constitution of the individual.

Nearly all men are born with certain predispositions, of which their physiognomy bears the stamp. Out of a hundred persons who die of consumption, ninety have brown hair, long faces, and pointed noses. Out of a hundred obese persons, on the other hand, ninety have short faces, round eyes, and snub noses.

It is certain therefore that there are persons virtually doomed as it were to corpulence, persons whose digestive activities, all things being equal, create more fat than those of their fellows.

This physical truth, of which I am firmly convinced, sometimes influences my way of looking at things in a most unfortunate manner.

When there appears in society a vivacious, pink-cheeked young person, with a pert nose, rounded contours, and short plump hands and feet, everybody is entranced and finds her charming; everyone, that is, but I. For, taught by experience, I look at her with eyes of twelve years hence, see the ravages which obesity will have wrought on those fresh young charms, and groan inwardly over ills so far non-existent. This anticipatory compassion is a painful sensation and furnishes one proof, among a thousand others, that man would be unhappier than he already is, if he could foresee the future.

The second of the chief causes of obesity is the floury and starchy substances which man makes the prime ingredients of his daily nourishment. As we have said already, all animals that live on farinaceous food grow fat willy-nilly; and man is no exception to the universal law.

Starch produces its effect sooner and more surely in conjunction with sugar; sugar and fat both contain hydrogen as a common element; both are inflammable. With this addition, it is the more active in that it pleases the palate more, and because sweet dishes are seldom eaten until the natural appetite has already been satisfied, when only that luxury appetite remains which must be coaxed by the most refined art and the subtlest variety.

Starch is no less fattening when conveyed in drinks, such as beer and other beverages of the same kind. The beer-drinking countries are also those where the biggest bellies are found; and certain Parisian families which, in 1817, drank beer for reasons of economy, were rewarded with paunches which they scarcely know what to do with.

CONTINUED

A dual cause of obesity results from excess of sleep and want of exercise.

The human body gains a great deal during sleep, and loses very little in the same period, since muscular activity is suspended. It thus becomes essential for the surplus acquired to be reduced by exercise; yet the time for activity is reduced in direct proportion to the time spent in sleep.

By another necessary consequence, heavy sleepers shun everything that promises to be at all tiring; the excess products of assimilation are therefore swept away by the torrent of circulation; they are there charged, by a process of which Nature alone holds the secret, with a little more hydrogen, and fat soon forms, to be deposited by the same agency in the capsules of the cellular tissue.

CONTINUED

A last cause of obesity consists of excessive eating and drinking.

We have had occasion to say that it is one of the privileges of mankind to eat without being hungry and drink without being thirsty; and indeed it cannot be a privilege shared by the animals, for it is born of reflection on the pleasures of the table, and the desire to prolong them.

This dual inclination has been found wherever men exist; and it is well known that savages eat to excess and drink themselves into a stupor whenever an opportunity presents itself.

As for ourselves, the citizens of the two worlds, who believe that we stand at the summit of civilization, it is certain that we eat too much.

I am not speaking of the few who, for reasons of avarice or impotence, live alone and apart; the former gloating over the money they are saving, the latter lamenting their inability to do better; I am speaking of all those who, moving about us, are in turn hosts or guests, politely offering or complaisantly accepting; who, when all their needs are satisfied, eat a dish because it is attractive, or drink a wine because it is new to them: I insist that whether they sit every day in fine dining-rooms or only celebrate Sundays and occasionally Mondays, the vast majority eat and drink too much, and huge quantities of food are absorbed every day without need.

This cause, almost always present, acts differently

according to the constitution of the individual; and in the case of those who have bad stomachs, its effect is not obesity, but indigestion.

ANECDOTE

We have witnessed with our own eyes an example which half Paris had the opportunity of observing.

Monsieur Lang had one of the most luxurious houses in that city; his table especially was excellent, but his stomach was as bad as his gourmandism was extreme. He did the honours perfectly, and himself ate with a courage worthy of a better fate.

Everything would go well until after the coffee; but soon his stomach would refuse to do its duty, pains would begin, and the wretched gastronome would be forced to throw himself down on a sofa and remain there till next day, expiating the brief pleasures he had tasted in prolonged anguish.

The remarkable thing is that he never changed his ways; as long as he lived, he freely accepted this strange alternation; and never allowed the sufferings of the evening to interfere with next day's dinner.

In the case of those whose stomach is in good shape, overeating acts as described in the previous chapter. Everything is digested and what is not needed for the body's recuperation solidifies and turns into fat.

With the others, chronic indigestion is the rule; their food passes through them without benefiting them, and those who are unaware of the reason are surprised when so many good things fail to produce better results.

It will be seen that I am not dealing exhaustively with the subject; for there are a thousand secondary causes arising out of our habits, occupations, enthusiasms, and pleasures which aid and abet those I have just mentioned.

All of this I bequeath to the successor I planted at the beginning of this chapter, contenting myself with that prelibation which belongs by right to first comers in every sphere.

It is a long time since intemperance first claimed the attention of observers. Philosophers have praised temperance, princes have made sumptuary laws, religion has moralized over gourmandism; but alas, not a mouthful the less has been eaten as a result, and the art of overeating flourishes more and more every day.

Perhaps I shall meet with better luck if I follow a new course; I intend to expose the *physical disadvantages of obesity*; self-preservation will perhaps be a stronger force than morals, more persuasive than sermons, more powerful than laws; for the fair sex, I believe, is quite prepared to open its eyes to the light.

DISADVANTAGES OF OBESITY

Obesity has an unfortunate effect on both sexes since it injures both strength and beauty.

It injures strength because, while increasing the weight of the mass to be moved, it does not increase the motive power; it is also harmful in that it obstructs breathing, and so makes any work impossible which demands the prolonged use of muscular energy.

Obesity injures beauty by destroying the originally established harmony of proportion; because all parts of the body do not fatten equally.

It also injures it by filling up the hollows which are Nature's shading; thus it is all too common to see faces which were once extremely attractive made almost plain by obesity.

The head of the late government did not escape the effects of this law. He grew extremely fat in the course of his last campaigns; his complexion turned from pale to ashen, and his eyes lost part of their proud fire.

Obesity brings with it a distaste for dancing, walking, and riding, and an inaptitude for every occupation or amusement requiring some degree of agility or skill.

It also opens the way for various diseases, such as apoplexy, dropsy, and ulcers of the legs, and makes all other ailments more difficult to cure.

EXAMPLES OF OBESITY

Of heroes who were corpulent, I can remember none but Marius and John Sobieski.

Marius, who was a short man, became as round as he was long, and it may have been his very enormity which terrified the Cimbrian charged with the duty of slaying him.

As for the King of Poland, his obesity came close to being the end of him; for, being forced to flee from a large body of Turkish cavalry, his breath soon failed him, and he would undoubtedly have been done to death if some of his aides-de-camp had not supported him, half unconscious, in his saddle, while others nobly sacrificed their lives to check the enemy.

If I am not mistaken, the Duc de Vendôme, that worthy son of the great Henri, was also a man of remarkable corpulence. He died at an inn forsaken by one and all, and retained enough consciousness to see the last of his servants snatch the cushion from under his head, just as he was giving up the ghost.

History provides many other instances of monstrous obesity; I shall pass over them, to speak a few words of those I have observed with my own eyes.

Monsieur Rameau, my schoolfellow as a boy and later Mayor of La Chaleur, in Burgundy, was only five feet two inches tall, and weighed five hundred pounds.

Monsieur le Duc de Luynes, beside whom I have often sat at table, became enormous; fat completely ruined his once elegant figure and he spent the last years of his life in a state of almost permanent somnolence.

But the most extraordinary example of this kind I ever saw was a citizen of New York, whom many Frenchmen still alive in Paris may have seen in the street called Broadway, sitting in a huge armchair the legs of which would have supported a church.

Edward was at least five feet ten inches tall, and as fat had blown him out in all directions, he was at least eight feet round. His fingers were like those of that Roman Emperor who used his wife's necklaces as rings; his arms and thighs were tubular, and as thick as an ordinary man's body; and he had feet like an elephant's, half hidden under the flesh of his legs; the weight of fat had drawn his lower eyelids down; but what made him hideous to behold was three spheroidal chins, which hung down for more than a foot over his chest, so that his face looked like the capital of a wreathed column.

In this condition Edward spent his life sitting at the window of a ground-floor room which looked out on to the street, every now and then drinking a glass of ale, a huge pitcher of which was always by his side.

Such an extraordinary figure could not fail to bring passers-by to a halt; but they were not allowed to linger, for Edward soon put them to flight, exclaiming in sepulchral tones: 'What are you staring at me for, like so many wild cats? . . . Get along with you, you lazy body . . . Be gone, you good for nothing dogs!' and other similar compliments.

I often used to greet him by name, and sometimes stopped for a chat; he assured me that he was neither bored nor unhappy, and that provided death did not disturb him, he would gladly await the end of the world in this fashion.

From what has been said in this chapter it is clear that if obesity is not a disease, it is at least an unfortunate indisposition, into which we nearly always fall through out own fault.

It is also clear that all must wish to avoid it if they are not already afflicted by it, and to be rid of it if they are.

On Restaurateurs

A restaurateur is a person whose trade consists in offering to the public an ever-ready feast, the dishes of which are served in separate portions, at fixed prices, at the request of each consumer.

The establishment is called a *restaurant*, and the person in charge of it the *restaurateur*. The list of dishes, bearing the name and price of each, is called the *carte*, or bill of fare, while the record of the dishes served to the customer, together with the relevant prices, is called the *carte à payer*, or bill.

Few among the crowds which patronize our restaurants every day pause to think that the man who founded the first restaurant must have been a genius endowed with profound insight into human nature.

We shall therefore aid the process of reflection and follow the thread of ideas which gave rise to this most popular and convenient institution.

ORIGIN

About 1770, after the glorious days of Louis XIV, the intrigues of the Regency, and the long and peaceful ministry of Cardinal Fleury, the visitor to Paris still found few resources in the way of good cheer.

He was forced to have recourse to the fare provided

by his innkeeper, which was generally bad. There were one or two hotels boasting a *table d'hôte*, but with few exceptions they offered only the barest necessities, and moreover served their meals at a fixed hour.

The visitor, it is true, could fall back on caterers; but they only supplied complete meals, and anyone who wished to entertain a few friends was obliged to order his requirements in advance; so that the stranger who had not the good fortune to be invited to dine at some rich house would leave our capital in total ignorance of the resources and delights of French cookery.

An order of things harmful to such everyday interests could not last; and already there were a few thinking men who dreamed of a change for the better.

At last a man of judgement appeared who decided that an active cause could not remain without effect; that with the same need recurring every day about the same times, consumers would flock to a place where they could be certain of that need being pleasantly satisfied; that if a wing of chicken were detached in favour of the first comer, a second would be sure to arrive who would be content with the leg; that the removal of a first slice in the obscurity of the kitchen would not put the remainder of the joint to shame; that nobody would mind a slight increase in price when they had received good, prompt, clean service; that if each guest were able to quibble over the price and quality of the dishes he ordered, there would be no end to the inevitable difficulties of the undertaking, but that a variety of dishes, combined with fixed prices, would have the advantage of suiting all purses.

This man thought of many other things, as may easily be imagined. He was the first restaurateur, and created a profession which is bound to make the fortune of anyone who exercises it with good faith, order, and ability.

ADVANTAGES OF THE RESTAURANT

The advent of the restaurant, which was adopted first by France, has proved a boon to all citizens, and of great importance to the culinary art.

1. By this means, a man may dine at whatever hour suits him, according to the circumstances in which he is placed by his business or pleasure;
2. He can be sure of not going beyond the sum which he thinks fit to spend on his meal, for he knows the price of every dish beforehand;
3. Having once come to a reckoning with his purse, the consumer may indulge at will in a light, heavy, or exotic meal, wash it down with the best French or foreign wines, flavour it with coffee, and perfume it with the liqueurs of both worlds, and all with no limit but the vigour of his appetite or the capacity of his stomach. The restaurant is the gourmand's paradise;
4. It is also a boon for the traveller, the foreigner, the man whose family is temporarily staying in the country, and for all, in a word, who have no cooking facilities at home, or are temporarily deprived of them.

Up to the date we mentioned above (1770), the rich and powerful had almost a monopoly of two great advantages: they alone travelled rapidly, and they alone constantly enjoyed good cheer.

With the advent of the new coaches which cover fifty leagues in twenty-four hours, the first of these privileges has disappeared; the advent of the restaurateur has destroyed the second; thanks to him, good cheer has become generally available.

Anyone with fifteen or twenty pistoles at his disposal, who sits down at the table of a first-class restaurateur, eats as well and even better than if he were at the table of a prince; for the feast which is offered him is just as splendid, and moreover, having every conceivable dish at his command, he is undisturbed by any personal consideration.

A RESTAURANT EXAMINED

The interior of a restaurant, examined in some detail, offers to the keen eye of the philosopher a spectacle well worth his interest, on account of the variety of situations contained within it.

The far end of the room is occupied by a host of solitary diners, who order loudly, wait impatiently, eat rapidly, pay, and depart.

At another table is a family from the country, content with a frugal meal, yet relishing one or two unfamiliar dishes, and obviously enjoying the novelty of their surroundings.

Nearby sit a husband and wife, Parisians, from the evidence of the hat and shawl hanging above their heads;

it is clearly a long time since they had anything to say to each other; they are going to the theatre, and it is a safe bet that one of them will fall asleep during the performance.

Farther on are two lovers, judging by the attentions of one, the coquetry of the other, and the gourmandism of both. Pleasure shines in their eyes; and, from the choice that governs the composition of their meal, the present serves both to illuminate the past and foreshadow the future.

In the centre of the room is a table surrounded by regular patrons, who as a rule obtain special terms, and dine at a fixed price. They know the names of all the waiters, who let them into the secret of what is freshest and newest; they are like the stock-in-trade of a shop, like a centre of attraction, or to be more precise, like the decoys used in Brittany to attract wild duck.

There are also a number of those individuals whom everyone knows by sight, and no one by name. These people are as much at ease as if they were at home, and quite often try to strike up a conversation with their neighbours. They belong to a type only met with in Paris, which has neither property, capital, nor employment, but spends freely for all that.

Finally, there are one or two foreigners, usually Englishmen; these last stuff themselves with double portions, order all the most expensive dishes, drink the headiest wines, and do not always leave without assistance.

The accuracy of our description may be verified any day of the week; and if it succeeds in rousing curiosity, perhaps it may also serve as a moral warning.

DISADVANTAGES

There can be no doubt that the availability and attraction of the restaurateur's wares may lead many people to indulge themselves beyond the limit of their faculties, and that this may cause indigestion, in the case of delicate stomachs, and some untimely sacrifices to the basest of Venuses.

But what is far more dangerous in our opinion to the social order is the fact that solitary reflection breeds egoism, by accustoming the individual to consider no one but himself, to hold aloof from his surroundings, and to show no consideration for others; and from their behaviour before, during, and after meals, it is an easy matter, in ordinary society, to single out from a party of guests those who normally eat in restaurants.*

RIVALRY

We have said that the advent of the restaurateur proved of great importance to the culinary art.

In fact, as soon as experience showed that a well-made *ragoût* was enough to make its inventor's fortune, self-interest, that most powerful of incentives, kindled every imagination and set every cook to work.

Analysis has revealed edible parts in substances formerly considered worthless; new foodstuffs have been

* Among other things, when a dish of ready-cut food is being handed round, they help themselves and put it down in front of them, without passing it to the neighbour whose needs they are unaccustomed to considering.

discovered, the old ones improved, and both combined in a thousand variations. Foreign inventions have been imported, and the whole world laid under contribution, until a single meal may constitute a complete course of alimentary geography.

FIXED-PRICE RESTAURANTS

While the culinary art thus rose to higher flights, in point of price as of discovery (for novelty must always be paid for), the same motive, namely the hope of gain, impelled it in the opposite direction, at least in the matter of expense.

Certain restaurateurs made it their aim to combine good cheer with economy, and by catering for modest incomes, which necessarily predominate, to make sure of attracting large numbers.

They sought out, among inexpensive substances, those which by skilful preparation could be made reasonably appetizing.

They found inexhaustible resources in the form of meat, which in Paris is always good, and salt-water fish, of which there is never a shortage; and by way of complement, there were fruit and vegetables, made cheaper by the latest methods of cultivation. They calculated what was strictly necessary to fill a stomach of ordinary capacity, and to quench any but an abnormal thirst.

They observed that there are many foods which owe their excessive price only to novelty or the time of year, but which can be supplied a little later, when this obstacle has ceased to exist; and in the end they reached a point when, at a profit of twenty-five to thirty per cent, they were able to offer their customers, for two francs or even less, an ample dinner, and one which any gentleman can be content with, since it would cost at least a thousand francs a month to maintain a table so well and variously furnished in a private house.

From this point of view, the restaurateur may be said to have rendered a signal service to that important part of the population of any great city which consists of foreigners, military men, and clerks; he was led by his own self-interest to the solution of a problem apparently contrary to it, namely, how to make good cheer available at a moderate price, and even cheaply.

The restaurateurs who have followed this course have been just as richly rewarded as their colleagues at the opposite end of the scale; they have met with fewer reverses, and their fortune, though slower to materialize, is far surer, for if they make a smaller profit, they make it every day, and it is a mathematical truism that when an equal number of units are brought together at a given point, they produce an equal total, whether they are brought together by tens, or one by one.

Connoisseurs still recall the names of several artists who have shone in Paris since the invention of the restaurant: names such as Beauvilliers, Méot, Robert, Rose, Legacque, the brothers Véry, Henneveu, and Baleine.

Some of these establishments owed their prosperity to special causes: for example, the Veau Qui Tette to sheep's trotters; the — to grilled tripe; the Frères Provençaux to cod cooked with garlic; Véry to truffled entrées; Robert to dinners ordered in advance; Baleine to the care he took to procure excellent fish; and Henneveu to the mysterious private rooms on his fourth floor. But of all these heroes of gastronomy, none has more right to a biographical notice than Beauvilliers, whose death was announced in the newspapers of 1820.

BEAUVILLIERS

Beauvilliers, who set up in business in 1782, was for more than fifteen years the most famous restaurateur in Paris.

He was the first to combine an elegant dining-room, smart waiters, and a choice cellar with superior cooking; and when several of the restaurateurs we have mentioned above tried to equal him, he never lost ground to them, because he had only a few steps to take to keep level with the progress of the art.

During the two successive occupations of Paris, in 1814 and 1815, vehicles of all nations were constantly at his door; he knew all the heads of foreign contingents, and learned to speak all their languages as well as was necessary for his business.

Towards the end of his life, Beauvilliers published a work in two octavo volumes, entitled *The Art of Cookery*. This work, the fruit of long experience, bears the seal of enlightened practice, and still commands the same respect it was accorded on its first appearance. Never before had the culinary art been expounded with such method and accuracy. This book, which has run into several editions, considerably simplified the task of writing the various works which have succeeded, but never surpassed it.

Beauvilliers was the possessor of a prodigious memory; he could recognize and greet, after an interval of twenty years, persons who had only eaten once or twice in his establishment. In certain cases he also had a method of procedure peculiar to himself. When he was told that a party of wealthy people had sat down at one of his tables, he would approach them with an obliging air, kiss the ladies' hands, and appear to honour his guests with special attention.

He would point out here a dish to be avoided and there one to be ordered at once, before it was too late; a third which nobody dreamed of ordering, he would order himself, at the same time sending for wine from a cellar to which he alone had the key; in a word, he assumed so gracious and engaging a tone, that all these additional items seemed so many favours on his part. But this amphitryonic role lasted only a moment; having played it, he withdrew from the scene; and before long the swollen bill, and the bitterness of Rabelais's quarter of an hour, amply demonstrated the difference between a host and a restaurateur.

Beauvilliers made his fortune, unmade it, and made it again several times over; we do not know in what circumstances death overtook him; but his tastes were so extravagant that we do not think his heirs can have inherited a great fortune.

THE GASTRONOME IN THE RESTAURANT

It will be found, on examining the bill of fare at various leading restaurants, notably those of the Véry brothers and the Frères Provençaux, that anyone who patronizes such an establishment has a choice, for the elements of his dinner, of at least

12 soups,
24 *hors-d'œuvre*,
15 or 20 beef entrées,
20 mutton entrées,
30 chicken or game entrées,
16 or 20 veal dishes,
12 pastry dishes,
24 fish dishes,
15 roasts,
50 side dishes,
50 dessert dishes.

In addition, the fortunate gastronome can wash his meal down with at least thirty kinds of wine, from Burgundy to Cape wine and Tokay, and with twenty to thirty kinds of liqueur, not to mention coffee and mixed drinks, such as punch, negus, syllabub, and the like.

Of these various component parts of a connoisseur's dinner, the principal parts are of French origin, such as the meat, fowl, and fruit; some are imitated from the English, such as beef-steak, Welsh rarebit, punch, etc., some come from Germany, such as the sauerkraut, Hamburg smoked beef, Black Forest fillets; some from Spain, such as the *olla podrida*, *garbanços*, Malaga raisins, Xerica pepper-cured ham, and dessert wines; some from Italy, such as the macaroni, Parmesan cheese, Bologna sausages, polenta, ices, and liqueurs; some from Russia, such as the dried meat, smoked eels, and caviare; some from

Holland, such as the salt cod, cheeses, pickled herring, curaçao, and anisette; some from Asia, such as the Indian rice, sago, curry, soy, Schiraz wine, and coffee; some from Africa, such as the Cape wines; and lastly, some from America, such as the potatoes, pineapples, chocolate, vanilla, sugar, etc.; all of which provides sufficient proof of the statement we have made elsewhere: that a meal such as may be had in Paris is a cosmopolitan whole, in which every part of the world is represented by its products.

Pheasant

The pheasant is an enigma, the answer to which is revealed only to the initiate; they alone can savour it in all its excellence.

Every substance has its esculent apogee; some attain it before they reach their full development, such as capers, asparagus, grey partridges, spoon-fed pigeons, etc.; some when they reach their natural prime, such as melons, most kinds of fruit, mutton, beef, venison, and red partridges; and some when they begin to decompose, such as medlars, woodcock, and, above all, pheasant.

This last bird, eaten within three days of its death, has an undistinguished taste. It is neither as delicate as a fowl, nor as fragrant as a quail.

Cooked at the right time, its flesh is tender, sublime, and tasty, for it partakes of both poultry and venison.

This desirable stage is reached just as the pheasant begins to decompose; only then does its fragrance develop, combining with an oil which, to be formed, requires a period of fermentation, like the oil of coffee, which is only obtained by roasting.

This moment is made manifest to the senses of the profane by a faint odour, and by a change in the bird's belly; but the inspired few divine it by a sort of instinct which moves them on certain occasions, as, for example, when a skilled cook decides at a glance to take a fowl from the spit or to leave it for a few more turns.

As soon as the pheasant has reached this stage, but no sooner, it is plucked and carefully larded with the freshest and crispest bacon.

It is not for nothing that we say that the pheasant must not be plucked too soon; careful experiments have shown that those kept in feather are much more fragrant than those which have been kept plucked for a long time, either because contact with the air neutralizes part of the flavour, or because a part of the juice which nourishes the feathers is reabsorbed, and helps to enrich the flesh.

After the bird has been plucked and larded, it is now ready to be stuffed; and this is done in the following way:

Have ready a brace of woodcock; bone and draw them, laying the liver and entrails on one side and the flesh on the other.

Take the flesh, and mince it with steamed ox-marrow, a little grated bacon, pepper, salt, herbs, and a sufficient quantity of good truffles to produce enough stuffing to fill the interior of the pheasant.

You will be careful to insert the stuffing in such a way that it cannot escape; quite a difficult business sometimes, when the bird is fairly high. There are various methods, however, one of which is to tie a crust of bread over the opening with a piece of thread, so that it serves as a stopper.

Then cut a slice of bread two inches longer at each end than the pheasant laid lengthwise; take the woodcocks' livers and entrails, and pound with two large truffles, an anchovy, a little grated bacon, and a piece of good fresh butter.

Spread this paste evenly over the bread, and place it beneath the pheasant prepared as above, so that it is thoroughly soaked with all the juice which exudes from the bird while it is roasting.

When the pheasant is cooked, serve it up gracefully reclining on its bed of toast; surround it with bitter oranges, and have no fear of the result.

This savoury dish is best washed down with good wine from Upper Burgundy; I derived this truth from a series of observations which cost me more trouble than a table of logarithms.

A pheasant cooked in this way would be worthy to set before angels, if they still walked the earth as in the days of Lot.

But what am I saying? The thing has been done. A stuffed pheasant was prepared before my very eyes by the good chef Picard, at the Château de la Grange, the home of my charming friend Madame de Ville-Plaine, and carried to the table by her steward Louis, stepping with processional dignity. It was as carefully scrutinized as one of Madame Herbault's hats; it was studiously savoured; and throughout this learned work the ladies' eyes shone like stars, their lips gleamed like coral, and their faces were pictures of ecstasy. (See my *Gastronomical Tests*.)

I have done more: I have offered such a dish to a group of judges of the Supreme Court, who know that it is sometimes necessary to lay aside the senatorial toga, and to whom I proved without much trouble that good cheer is Nature's compensation for the cares of the bench.

After careful consideration the President announced in a grave voice the word *Excellent!* All heads bowed in agreement, and the verdict was unanimous.

I had observed, during the period of deliberation, that the noses of those venerable men were agitated by marked olfactory twitchings, that their august brows shone with calm serenity, and that about the corners of each judicial mouth there played something which might almost have been a smile.

But these remarkable effects are in the nature of things. For a pheasant cooked in accordance with the foregoing recipe, already distinguished enough in itself, is impregnated from outside by the savoury juices of the roasting bacon, while from inside it absorbs the fragrant gases given off by the woodcock and truffles. Meanwhile, the toast, richly garnished already, is also soaked with the three varieties of gravy which exude from the roasting bird.

Thus of all the good things brought together, not a single particle escapes appreciation; and such is the virtue of this dish that I consider it worthy of the most august of tables.

*Parve, nec invideo, sine me liber ibis in aulam.**

---

* 'Little book, you'll go without me to the palace, nor do I grudge you this.' [Ed.]

GREAT  FOOD

THROUGHOUT the history of civilization, food has been livelihood, status symbol, entertainment – and passion. The twenty fine food writers here, reflecting on different cuisines from across the centuries and around the globe, have influenced each other and continue to influence us today, opening the door to the wonders of every kitchen.

THE WELL-KEPT KITCHEN..Gervase Markham

THE JOYS OF EXCESS ....Samuel Pepys

EVERLASTING SYLLABUB AND THE ART OF CARVING..........Hannah Glasse

RECIPES FROM THE WHITE HART INN...William Verrall

A DISSERTATION UPON ROAST PIG & Other Essays.....................Charles Lamb

THE PLEASURES OF THE TABLE ....Brillat-Savarin

THE ELEGANT ECONOMIST ....Eliza Acton

THE CHEF AT WAR...Alexis Soyer

THE CAMPAIGN FOR DOMESTIC HAPPINESS...........................Isabella Beeton

NOTES FROM MADRAS .... Colonel Wyvern

EXCITING FOOD FOR SOUTHERN TYPES................................Pellegrino Artusi

FROM ABSINTHE TO ZEST ....Alexandre Dumas

BUFFALO CAKE AND INDIAN PUDDING...................................Dr A. W. Chase

A LITTLE DINNER BEFORE THE PLAY ....Agnes Jekyll

MURDER IN THE KITCHEN...Alice B. Toklas

LOVE IN A DISH & Other Pieces ....M. F. K. Fisher

A TASTE OF THE SUN ....Elizabeth David

A MIDDLE EASTERN FEAST..Claudia Roden

EATING WITH THE PILGRIMS & Other Pieces ....Calvin Trillin

RECIPES AND LESSONS FROM A DELICIOUS
   COOKING REVOLUTION ....Alice Waters